ABDALL.

FIGHT

confronting evil.
escaping darkness.

All Scripture references are from the New American Standard Bible, and used by permission of The Lockman Foundation, printed by Moody Bible Institute of Chicago, 1976, 1978.

ISBN PRINT: 9781702114981

Cover Design and Interior Book Design by Sarah O'Neal | eve custom artwork
Interior Images are available online/Public Domain

AVAILABLE ON AMAZON

NOTE FROM THE AUTHOR: All the events in this story are true, although some of the names have been altered to protect the lives of people who have significantly influenced my life.

It is the LORD who goes before you.
You need not be afraid.

DEUTERONOMY 31:8

DEDICATION

I want to dedicate this book to all the hurting children around the world

To those who are suffering from violence, abuse, and intolerance of war,

To those who had their voices and screams silenced by the sound of gunfire and bombs,

To those who have had their dreams shattered by war, poverty and deprivation,

To those who are robbed of their innocence and are forced to become grown-ups at an early age...

To all those who are hurting, and fighting not to lose hope in life.

I want to dedicate this to my sons, Pedro and Daniel

You are the reason I've done all that I have done. I wanted to bring you to a place without war, a place of security, safety and freedom, a place where you can live without fear and uncertainty of tomorrow... a place where you can have a better life and a much better future. I am so thankful that my children don't have to experience all the terrible things I had to go through.

I want this book to be a reminder for my children and others to stand up against evil and violence. Use your voice and your freedom to help other kids who are hurting and suffering around the world.

I also want to dedicate this book to my loving parents

You sacrificed yourselves to protect and provide for us. You demonstrated ultimate sacrifice and unconditional love during the worst of times. I am forever grateful to you both and will never forget what you have done for me.

Finally, I want to dedicate this book to the many friends and all the innocent people who lost their lives during the vicious war in Lebanon.

You will always be remembered.

CONTENTS

FIGHT

A true story of the lifelong journey of a young boy

filled with pain, hurt, tragedy, sorrow, struggle... and victory

This book contains disturbing images, reader discretion is advised

prologue

Dark Black

IT'S DARK. BLACK. COLD. At six years old, I curl up tight on my thin mat with my thin blanket, trying to get warm, trying to take up as little space as possible in the corner of my family's bunker... trying to go to sleep with the sounds of bombs and machine guns disturbing the night. Weariness from the constant fear – rather than true peaceful rest – finally overcomes me, and my eyes close.

Immediately, I hear thuds and a splintered crash, as a group of men in masks kick in the wooden door and storm into our bunker. A couple of them stand guard at the door – whether it's to keep us in, or keep others out, I do not know. One has a flashlight, and the thin beam of light sweeps and flicks around the room, capturing the confused and terrified faces of my family, and for a brief moment, highlighting the masked intruders. By the quick glimpses of their clothes and weapons, I know them as Palestinian fighters. With a knife in one hand, and a machine gun in the other hand, one of them forces us to all kneel down... almost all of us, anyway. I'm the only one he doesn't see, curled up in the corner, hiding under my blanket. I pull the blanket closer over my head and don't dare to breathe.

The flashlight is not a comfort; it acts more like a weapon, aiding the faceless enemies in their violence. They have my whole family on their knees with the machine guns pointed at them. And then, one by one, they slaughter them. One man starts with my mom, aiming at her head, coldly ignoring her tears and desperate pleas for her children. Then he shoots my dad, and then each of my brothers, one by one. All their bodies crumple to the concrete floor, and blood is everywhere – spattered on my face and on the walls and running across the floor toward me. I smell the gunpowder, and the stench of death mixes with the mildew of the cold, damp bunker – this coffin, where we will all be buried alive and forgotten.

Then he grabs my four-year-old sister by her hair. He's saved her for last. With the knife, he grazes across her neck without cutting her - the first time, the second time, the third time. She is panicked and terrified, gasping and sobbing. He must have known I was there, because this seems to be a special torture, designed just for me. Even though his face is behind a mask, I can see that his eyes blaze with hate. Why did he hate us so much? What had my family done to him? I don't want to watch anymore, don't want to smell the blood or hear my sister cry, don't want to see him slaughter her like a helpless, innocent lamb. But I cannot look away. I try to fight, and I want to scream, but my arms won't move, and no sound comes out...

His knife presses against my sister's neck, until I jump up, screaming in the middle of the night, scaring everybody in the bunker - my mom, my dad, my brothers, my sister. And in the dark black, I do not see the blazing eyes anymore. I want to believe he is not really there, but I can never know for certain.

Whenever I woke from these night terrors as a child, my mom would sit with me for an hour or so. I hated that she tried to settle me down to sleep again.

"I don't want to go back to sleep!" I would cry into her shoulder. "I don't want to, because this nightmare will continue if I go back to sleep. If this one doesn't continue, I'm just going to have another nightmare, and I don't want that!"

My mom held me tight, and her loving, gentle words helped me through the night: "You're going to be OK, Aboudi. I will not let anything bad happen to you..." Then she'd spend a couple hours with me in the freezing cold, singing and praying for me until I fell asleep again.

I was six years old. The nightmares haunted me for almost sixteen years of my life.

The reality was, that whether I was awake or asleep, the nightmare continued. It was the world I lived in: men with guns and knives, innocent victims killed, fear and darkness. Throughout that time, I told myself, "I don't want to live anymore. I want to end my life. I want to stop this misery because this is too much to handle. I'm struggling a lot, I'm hurting a lot, and I'm not seeing anything that's getting better."

There's no such thing as hope, you know. At least, that is what I believed at a very young age. Once you see just a tiny little window that looks like hope, you think, "OK, this is worth living for. I want to continue living!" But whichever way I lived my childhood, I didn't see any windows of hope - everything was shut.

It's dark. Black. Cold. It's like being in a dark black hole with no openings. Wherever I looked - darkness. I didn't see anything but black.

FIGHT
confronting evil.
escaping darkness.

chapter 1

The Bunker Years

My parents had a huge house, but we didn't live in it very much. My early years were "bunker years" – that's what I remember. I used to think that there was nothing in life but the bunker and trying to survive another day.

We lived in a 10x10ft bunker, a bomb shelter. My father built it in 1970, before I was born, so I don't remember our home without it. It was in front of the house; we had to go out the front door and walk about 20 yards to get to it. The bunker was just plain, grey cement walls, with nothing else – no drywall, no paint, no floors, no windows, no lights... nothing.

I mean, it had thick walls and thick ceilings, and my dad bedded it with sand to make it stronger so that the bombs and the rockets wouldn't penetrate the bunker and kill us all. And it had a small wooden door that my dad made at the entrance. So we felt protected from the top and from the sides, but what would happen if somebody came in that door, or a bomb landed in front of the bunker and shrapnel got in? We would all be dead. So even with all these walls, this concrete, I felt naked and vulnerable.

My dad and mom used to store food for us. They stored as much food as possible, but they couldn't store any perishable food because we frequently

The Bunker

lost power for weeks, sometimes for months. There was no fridge, nothing to heat and nothing to cook on. It was too dangerous to go outside to cook, so we just ate whatever we could get our hands on, which was mostly old bread. And many times we didn't have anything to eat, and slept hungry. The only person who had the courage to go outside the bunker and go to the house to get us food or supplies was my dad. I used to look up to him and think, "What a brave man!" He was my hero for laying his life on the line, just to go home and get us something to eat.

All we had were candles and mattresses – thin, foam mattresses, not the fancy kind. The floor was damp, and smelled of mildew because it was underground. And it was so cold, especially in the winter nights - it felt like

I was outside in the North Pole, in the freezing wind, in only a thin shirt. I could feel the cold floor through my mattress. So we had to be creative, to do whatever we could to get warm. We each had our own mattresses, and our own place on the floor, but when it was so cold, we used to squeeze together, all of us gathered on two or three mattresses in one spot. That's how we generated heat, so we could stay warm at night.

Just imagine six kids with our parents – eight people in that tiny space! No matter what shape or form you try to fit, it doesn't work out so well.

My brothers and I would wrestle with each other and draw on the walls of the bunker. We drew with little rocks and pencils, if we had any available. Having a pencil or a crayon was a big deal. Most of our drawings were inspired by war, like soldiers in battle, machine guns, and superheroes.

We played games, but not the kind of games many little boys would play. We would listen to the gunshots and explosions outside, and guess how close the bombs landed, and what type of artillery it was, based on the sound.

But eventually – all too soon, at times - we got bored, and after too many days spent inside in the dark, my brothers and I got restless. So my dad would light some candles, enough for us to see his tired smile and a small glimmer in his eye, and he would say to us, "Did I ever tell you about the time when your uncle became the wrestling champion for the armies from around the world?"

We needed a distraction, so my dad told us stories. Sometimes it was about our ancestors who fought for many years to defend our small town from invaders. Sometimes it was fictional tales, and sometimes it was accounts of my father's life or his family. Of course, we had heard the one about Uncle Hayel's triumph a hundred times before, but we still loved it, so we pretended it was new, and begged him to tell us all the details. "He was up against this big, mean opponent, twice his size! It didn't look good for your uncle. And as he got thrown onto the mat. . ."

BOOM! We all jumped as the background rhythm of the war outside suddenly hit very close and we felt the earth shake around us. I looked at my dad in shock, and all I could see was his lips moving like he was shouting, his hands frantically pointing at the far corner of the bunker. I couldn't hear anything he was saying, but I ran to the corner and huddled with my brothers. I covered my ears and closed my eyes tight, trying to make myself disappear until it was over.

It took a few minutes for the ringing in my ears to stop, and then I could hear my brothers and sister scream and cry in terror, and I could hear my dad's words, which still echo in my ears to this day: "Get in the corner

quick, and hide! Don't be afraid! It will be over *soon*." I don't know why, but I trusted in those words, and I believed what my dad was saying. He was so strong; he was my rock.

For a few brief moments, we had been so caught up in the story that we imagined ourselves in a gym, surrounded by cheering fans, watching our uncle dance around on a mat, and we'd forgotten that we were in the midst of our own terrible fight. Inside, dust fell around us, and outside we could hear shouts and screams. Missiles rained down around our bunker and our neighborhood. I imagined myself in a wrestling ring, beaten, bruised, and bloody, slumping against the ropes like my uncle. Only, instead of Hayel's victorious comeback, I fell to the mat in defeat as my enemy mercilessly punished me, my family, and my community until we had nothing left.

Often the stories were left unfinished because we were all so scared and shaken by the attacks. The explosions hit so close – sometimes right next to our bunker. It is amazing that our whole family survived. But our neighbors weren't so lucky. One time, a missile hit their house, killing the mother and two other family members. Neighbors would come running to our bunker for shelter, and even though the space was so small and cramped for our family alone, it often provided a place of safety for up to fifteen people, for days at a time.

We lived like that until I was 20 years old.

In our town, there were a lot of stray dogs, but I especially remember one that used to hang around our house, that we named Lucy. She was sweet and beautiful, and very friendly and gentle with us. She sort of adopted me and my brothers as her family. My parents always loved Lucy and took good care of her. And anytime we went away, she would stay and protect our house.

Then she had a litter of four puppies. When our town was under attack, Lucy ran with her puppies and stood outside the door of our bunker, barking and howling, as if she were begging for permission to come inside. The puppies whined and squirmed, and their tiny innocent faces looked so scared and confused. I felt like I could hear them cry, "Won't you please let us in? We're frightened, and we don't want to die! We're too young to die!"

Too young to die... It was a plea that resounded in my own young heart as bombs exploded around me, destroying my home and everything precious about my childhood. I couldn't bear to listen to them on the other side of the door, hurting and feeling desperate and vulnerable like me. So

Me at age 8

I ran to the door and let them in. I had great respect for Lucy, and she thanked us wholeheartedly by licking our hands and faces one by one. "Thank you!" her relieved and happy expression said to us. "Thank you for giving us shelter and protecting my young ones!"

After things quieted down outside, she would take her puppies and leave. But they would return often, to play and cuddle. And we would keep the door cracked open for them to run inside whenever there was danger. They needed comfort, and so did we. I really felt like we helped each other through some of our darkest times.

Lucy died in one of the missile attacks. Her puppies were still only a few months old at that time. Losing her was devastating to all of us. I felt angry, as if the one thing that was helping me and giving me the comfort I desperately needed had been snatched away.

The water and power for the bunker used to come and go, come and go... We never knew when we're going to have power, we never knew when we were going to have drinking water, we never knew if we were going to have water to wash our clothes or wash ourselves – we just didn't know. One thing that disturbed my life the most was uncertainty.

When you live in uncertainty, you don't know what to think and when to think about anything. It's like you shouldn't have a plan for anything. You can't say, "Oh, today I am going to do this, this, this, and this, and tomorrow I am going to do this, this, and this..." No! You don't have a life. You just sit quietly and pray that you survive another day without being killed by a bomb or gunshot. That's how we had to live in South Lebanon. It wasn't just me; it was everybody who was living in South Lebanon.

It didn't make any sense... even though we had this protection – this bunker - we didn't feel protected. Something was missing. And that plagued me psychologically. I didn't know if I should feel secure or not. I wanted to sleep, but I didn't know if I should sleep, because maybe I should keep my eyes open in case something happened. And it wasn't just a day, or two days - sometimes we stayed for ten days, until we felt like we couldn't step outside because we knew that there was great danger. We knew that we were always vulnerable.

That sense of insecurity developed within me, grew with me as I got older. The bunker was our home underground, but I felt like we were buried alive. I wish I could erase all the terrible memories of hurt and pain, that my time in the bunker caused. I wish I could get back all my childhood years that were stolen from me and my brothers.

chapter 2
The Hills & Valleys of Life

MY FAMILY LIVED IN A SMALL TOWN in South Lebanon called El Qlaiaa, only about five kilometers from the Israeli border. The town is situated on top of a hill. In fact, that whole region of Lebanon is a series of hills and valleys, rolling over each other, rising higher and higher into the eastern mountain range which forms much of our natural border with Syria.

My Town

From the balcony of my parents' home, facing the east, we could see a beautiful green valley, and in the distance, Mount Hermon. This is the highest peak in Israel and Syria, and has great religious significance (as many things in that part of the world do) to Christian and Jewish people.

To the west is another valley and the Litani River, flowing southwest toward the Mediterranean Sea. Beyond the river, on another hill is the Belfort Castle, which was a Crusader fortress built in the 12th century. It has always been a very strategic place for military use: from the castle, there is a good view of northern Israel. During my childhood, the Palestinian army had control of it until the summer of 1982, when the Israeli army advanced and captured it.

On the hill to the north of El Qlaiaa is the city of Marjeyoun, which was the military headquarters for the South Lebanon Army during the war, and on the hill to the south is the small town of Bourj al Moulouk.

It's truly incredible, how much you can see on top of a hill that is about 2,300 feet above sea level. But I never traveled very far outside of my town when I was a child; it was just too dangerous. My world was very small – confined mostly to the bunker, the driveway, and the ten-minute walk to

school. There were no family vacations or field trips... no hikes up to the famous and historic castle, no camping trips down by the river. I viewed these beautiful things the same way I viewed my chance for freedom - from a great distance, across valleys that seemed more like giant chasms that were impossible to cross.

Though my living space was limited, I do have memories of it being full and rich with community. When I was a child, my town had around 5,000 people. We were all a big family, loving and caring for one another. People in my town didn't have phones, so they would meet in person to talk. Everybody was in each other's lives; they loved to socialize and spend time together. They took every opportunity to be together, for better or worse, through all the hills and valleys of life.

Every chance we had – and even then, only after a lot of begging – my brothers and I used to go down to the Litani River to play. We would swim for hours in that cold, clear water, that shimmered green in the reflection of the hills surrounding it. Our favorite game was to climb up on the rocks and cliffs, and jump or dive into the water.

I was about twelve years old, the first time I jumped. The rock was so high, and from that height I could see the shadows of huge rocks down in the water, forming a border around the small swimming hole where it was safe to jump. I shivered, partly from the cold drops of water on my bare skin, but mostly because I was scared. Those rocks in the water mesmerized me, and I couldn't help thinking, *"What if I miss, and land on those rocks!"* But to me, there was one thing worse than feeling afraid...

"Come on, slow poke! Just jump already! We don't have all day – we have to leave soon!" Walid urged me from behind. Joeseph and Jeel were down in the water, splashing and yelling up to me. Joeseph cheered me on: "You can do it, Abdallah!" But Jeel taunted me: "Yeah, what are you – a chicken?!" That was just what I needed to hear, spur me on; there was no way I would look like a coward in front of my brothers! I took a deep breath, shut my eyes, and jumped feet-first into the icy pool. As I splashed and swam to the surface, I could hear my brothers cheering – I had conquered my fear and gained a victory! From that time on, we challenged each other to jump from higher and higher places, sometimes fifteen or even twenty-five feet tall!

We also liked to fish, using spears and nets, and then we cleaned and cooked our fish over a small fire on the bank of the river. Some people came to the river with dynamite or hand grenades. We would quickly climb out of the water and watch from a safe distance while they threw dynamite into the river. A big explosion would send hundreds of fish flying twenty feet in the air, and then they fell back down, lifelessly smacking the surface of the water. Then the fishermen threw nets out over the surface, to collect and bring in the fish.

Even with all this fun, those trips to the river with my brothers were tainted with a constant fear and risk; we could easily get stuck in one area, unable to get to safety because of the fighting and ambushes on the roads, or worse – we could be kidnapped or killed. We stayed together and watched out for each other, and made sure we left early, in plenty of time to reach home before dark.

I remember the festivals and celebrations we had; even in the midst of war, holidays like Christmas, New Year, and Easter were happy times for us. During annual festivals, the streets were busy and bustling with excited people, lively music, fun games, and food... Oh, the food! Everybody made delicious things to eat at the festivals: fresh bread, grilled chicken, grilled pork, and beef, and there was plenty for all.

"Step right up, young men! Let's see how good your aim is!" A big man called to Jeel and me as we approached his simple wooden booth on the street. Behind him, all lined up along the back wall of the inside of the booth, was a row of old tin cans. He held out a tennis ball to me, coaxing me to play. "How many can you knock down?" he asked, pointing to the cans. I glared at them and threw the ball – got one! Another ball, and two more cans toppled over. In the end, I managed to hit seven out of the ten cans, which was not bad for a small boy.

Jeel patted me on the back, and the man in the booth gave me a fluffy little green stuffed bear. Such a small and silly prize, but I would give it to my sister and she would be thrilled. For me, the real prize was the joy of winning. I threw my arms in the air and whooped, then jumped and ran around like crazy, laughing and yelling, "Yes, I won! I won!" For once, I could celebrate overcoming an obstacle, a challenge, no matter how small and insignificant it was. In that moment, I wasn't the victim - I was the champion.

But sometimes I did not feel like a champion, and the people in my town did not gather to play games, but to comfort and help each other through personal struggles. Sometimes the struggles were work problems, and sometimes they were sicknesses or injuries. Many people cooked food for the families in need and visited them in their homes, giving advice or offering support, comfort, and prayers.

Sometimes I played soccer with my brothers and some of our friends in an empty lot between two houses in our neighborhood. One day while we were playing, we heard missiles exploding, so we abandoned our game and all ran back to our homes. My brothers and I were safe, but a bomb fell on one of the boy's houses and killed him and his mother. I remember how much his father and the rest of the family grieved after that, and my parents took food to them for two weeks, trying to help ease the pain of the horrific loss they had suffered. During the war, this sort of thing happened much too often, but people never stopped giving, serving, and loving each other.

And then, after the tears and food and visits and prayers, everybody would help to rebuild the town... whether it was houses, the church, or the school, the efforts of the whole community kept us patched up and held together. In this way, we were choosing to not live in despair, but fought for hope, after every single attack that came against us.

Wedding celebrations were a favorite way for our town to forget the terrible conditions of the war and the tragic losses we suffered over the years. Weddings meant new life, a new chapter, a new generation. They meant birth instead of death, unity instead of division, love instead of hate. And so we honored weddings and rejoiced in the hope that they brought to all of us.

For a whole week before the actual wedding day, people celebrated with parties every night. By the time they got to the wedding day, the bride and the groom were exhausted because of all the partying they had done!

A few hours before the wedding, the groom would be surrounded by a large crowd of people from town who had worked together to give him a clean shave and put a new suit on him. Then they put him on a chair, and lifted him up, making him dance up in the air as they sang and cheered.

Besides gifts, people also gave money to the new couple. A man with a recorder would receive all the money, and publicly shout the names of the people who gave the money and how much they gave: "Paul Saeed: 100,000 pounds!" And these kinds of announcements continued for almost an hour.

After the wedding ceremony, the newlywed couple would get in a convertible car, and a long line of cars of relatives and friends would follow behind them, driving around town, honking and cheering, forming a grand parade. People in town, young and old, would line up on both sides of the street and start throwing rice, flowers and candy at them. I enjoyed that so much, because my brother Jeel and I would compete to see who could collect more candy as it bounced off the cars and landed on the street; that's what I remember most about weddings when I was a little kid: parades and candy.

My town is known for its ancient olive trees, and for having the purest olive oil. During harvest season in November, families got together to help each other. Most of the gathering was done by hand, and people would lay out large sheets and blankets for collecting all the olives under the trees. Harvest season was another way for people to escape the war and keep their minds occupied.

I personally didn't enjoy it much, because I got bored very quickly. "Mom, I don't want to work!" I pleaded as we drove out to the orchards. "I want to go play, and breathe the fresh air!"

"You can breathe the fresh air and get good exercise by helping with the olives," she would point out. "Now you stay close where I can see you, Abdallah. And no more arguing!"

I wanted to be free with my brothers to run in the fields, without any walls or restrictions. But there were landmines hidden all over the fields, with no signs or barbwire to warn us. We might play in a landmine field and not even know it until it was too late. Many times, we heard about children who lost their limbs by stepping on landmines. It's hard to believe, but one minute we would be playing and having fun, and the next minute we were crying and traumatized by the deaths of our neighbors, our playmates... our friends.

I believe the war brought the people of my town even closer together. They stood by one another in times of crisis and stayed united against all odds. I don't remember any conflicts within our community; all we wanted, all we strived for, was to live in peace.

It is painful in some ways even to recall the best of times, because they all seem tainted with tragedy. It's as though I am looking at a beautiful painting, mesmerized and in awe of its vibrant colors, graceful strokes, and all the light and life it portrays. And just as I begin to relax and smile, and find comfort in that masterpiece, it begins to catch fire. The edges curl up as they are singed, holes burn through the canvas and grow bigger, soot dulls the color, and the smell of death creeps over it – the stench of gunpowder and burning flesh. And right before my eyes, this beautiful painting transforms into something gloomy and dark and ugly. That's how it felt, watching the beauty and joy in my world crumble, leaving behind only memories and vague shadows of what once was good.

It wasn't a stable life, with all these ups and downs. We worked so hard to reach the hilltops – the best and happiest times – and we fought so hard to embrace and enjoy them while they lasted, before they inevitably crashed into pain and loss. But from the depths of that darkness, we looked up again, gathering strength to get back up and start climbing to the heights once more.

I miss everything about my town. My parents still live in the same old house, and even though I had to go through a lot of hurt and suffering in my life, I still miss that home, where I have so many memories - the good and the bad.

I miss my community there - my parents, my friends, and my relatives. I miss the beautiful nature - the springs, the green hills, the fields, the trees,

My Family Home

the birds, and the amazing views. Now I live in America, and I'm thankful for the safety and freedom I have here. But nothing will ever be able to replace the love and longing I have for my home among the hills and valleys of Lebanon.

chapter 3

A Radio View of the World

JUNE 6, 1982: "BREAKING NEWS – Under the direction
of Defense Minister Ariel Sharon, Israeli forces are now
invading Southern Lebanon..."

MY DAD USED TO HAVE A SMALL RADIO, and that was our source for
everything; all the news that we got was from that battery-powered
radio. And even through the static and over the sounds of explosions
outside our bunker, we used to just sit together as a family and try to
listen.

I remember hearing a radio station from London that broadcasted in
Arabic from Greenwich, and that's the one that my dad used to listen to.
He just held the radio next to his ear, and we all surrounded him as close

19

as possible, to try to hear what was going on, as if we knew or were trying to make sense of it all, even though we didn't have a clue. He would break down the reports in a way that we could understand: "This is what's going to happen, you know, probably in the next week or so: we might be able to go outside, and we might be able to go back and spend a few days up in the house!" And we would breathe a sigh of relief.

When we heard the announcement about the Israeli invasion, we knew this would be a game-changer. Their plan was to drive the Palestinian Liberation Organization (PLO) forces out of South Lebanon, and that summer, they succeeded in pushing them all the way to Beirut. We didn't need to spend as much time in the bunker after Israel occupied South Lebanon, because they had more control over the Palestinians coming in and attacking and hurting and killing us, so there were fewer attacks. But that didn't mean the problems were over or that the violence in our town had come to an end.

When they entered our country, they had to pass through our town – the Israeli tanks and all the military convoys. As a child, I saw a huge tank rolling down the street... and then it was not just one, but more like twenty in a long line, one after another, in the nighttime, never during the day.

We would start running after the tanks, and Israeli soldiers on top of some of these tanks started throwing small bags of candy for us. All the kids in my neighborhood were fighting in the streets over who was going to catch the candy first. It was very dangerous, but we didn't fear the tanks. We didn't even think of the possibility of being run over by the huge machines that were only inches away from us - we were only interested in that bag of candy! It was our delicious evidence that surely, everything about life would be sweeter from now on.

Yasser Arafat, Palestinian Militant Leader

Palestinian Militants

Israeli Invasion of Lebanon

JUNE 19, 1982: "Israeli forces continue to surround Beirut, attacking by air, land, and sea, in a siege that has now lasted almost one week. The U.N. Security Council expresses deep concern at the situation for the civilian population of Beirut, and reaffirms its call for resolution, demanding the immediate withdrawal of Israeli forces from the city, as a first step toward withdrawal from the country of Lebanon..."

The summer of 1982 is probably the part of the Lebanese Civil War that the world remembers the most. On June 3, there was an assassination attempt on Israeli ambassador, Shlomo Argov, in London, England. In response, Israeli forces attacked the PLO in Lebanon.

The assassination attempt was not a solitary act of aggression. Israel had been under attack since the early 1970s from Palestinian forces in Lebanon, because the goal of the PLO was to conquer and take possession of the land of Israel. When the PLO launched enough missiles at Israel, Israel would fire back. Over the years, the United Nations Security Council would intervene, demanding mutual and simultaneous cease-fire in 1978, 1981, and in early 1982. Each time, Israel would stop fighting and withdraw.... until the next time the PLO attacked.

For about ten years Beirut, the Lebanese capital, was the PLO base of operations. The Palestinian and Syrian militaries occupied and gained power in that city, so much so that the official Lebanese government had very little control.

In response to the Israeli attack, and the subsequent counter-attack by the PLO in June, 1982, the UN once again called for a cease-fire. But this time, Israel did not comply. In fact, Israel advanced its forces into Lebanon, rather than retreat. Israel would not tolerate the aggression anymore, and

Yasser Arafat with his fighters

Palestinian Militants

Israeli Troops rolling into Lebanon

would not allow its neighbor, Lebanon, to be a launching stage for attacks against its people.

In the course of one week, 60,000 Israeli troops moved through Lebanon, advancing 40 kilometers to Beirut from three different directions. Their plan was to break the strongholds of the PLO and force them to withdraw their presence and power in Lebanon, establish a security zone along the southern border of Lebanon that would protect northern Israel from future missile attacks, and form a peace treaty alliance with the Lebanese government. Israel besieged Beirut in an effort to accomplish their goals as quickly as possible.

But the PLO and Syrian forces refused to leave, and the siege lasted for over three months, making that a very tense summer. Food, water, and electric supplies to the city were cut off, and constant attacks meant that there were heavy losses, military and civilian alike. The UN reaffirmed their demands for cease-fire and the withdrawal of Israeli troops over and over again – on June 18 and 19, July 4 and 29, and August 1, 4, 12, and 17 – but without any compliance. The United States vetoed the UN's demands, and actively worked to negotiate Israel's goals with the PLO, Syria, and the Lebanese government.

During that time, the entire country of Lebanon was in turmoil. There was so much fighting on all fronts, between so many different groups, but in my town we had already lived through so much that these extra battles were not very shocking to us. We had mixed feelings about the siege; we felt left behind by our own country and we didn't know whom to trust anymore. We didn't want anybody occupying our land; we just wanted to have our home back. We were all looking for a way out of the miserable situation we were in, and we didn't care who would do the job, as long as they brought an end to the suffering.

AUGUST 21, 1982: "An agreement has been reached and the first steps are being taken today to end the crisis and evacuate Palestinian forces from west Beirut. French Foreign Legion paratroops have landed in east Beirut and are the first of a multinational peacekeeping force that is to supervise the pullout. 800 U.S. marines will arrive in west Beirut later this week, to participate in a three-nation peacekeeping force. International allies of Lebanon believe the success of these actions will allow for the rapid departure of all foreign troops from the country..."

French troops led the way for multinational forces, including the U.S. Marines and Italian forces, to finally intervene, actively overseeing the withdrawal of PLO from Lebanon. Once this threat was pushed back, Israel were also forced to leave. We began to hope that we would be able to rebuild our country as an unoccupied, free, and peaceful nation.

Unfortunately, all of this did not take care of the problem. When the Israelis left Beirut, they created the Security Zone and left a part of the country occupied – our part of the country, South Lebanon. The South Lebanon Army was a group of former military who banded together to protect their homes and families. The people of South Lebanon were under the impression that they would be more protected with the presence of the Israeli Army and the South Lebanon Army from the radical militant attacks.

That wasn't the case. Things got even worse for us. More attacks, more bombings, more rocket attacks... the situation progressed as time went by, because other enemies advanced and attacked.

SEPTEMBER 15, 1982: "This morning Lebanese Prime Minister, Shafik Wazzan, confirmed the death of President-elect, Bachir Gemayel. Gemayel was assassinated yesterday when a bomb exploded at 4:10pm inside the Phalangists headquarters in Beirut..."

We all saw hope and a better future in Gemayel as our new President. He was working to end the war, striving for a peaceful resolution between Syria and Israel. Many people viewed him as our savior, and his presidency gave us some hope to end our struggle. My dad was furious when he heard the news of his assassination. He threw the radio across the bunker and it broke into pieces against the concrete walls and floor. "That was our only hope," he said wearily, "and now it is gone."

My father was not the only one who felt this way. All over the world – the world outside our little bunker, outside our little town, the world I had never seen and only knew through the static of our radio – people grieved and raged over this tragedy.

The American President Ronald Reagan had been a supporter and ally of Gemayel, and responded to the news of his death: *"...The news of the cowardly assassination of Bachir Gemayel, President-elect of Lebanon, is a shock to the American people and to civilized men and women everywhere. This promising young leader had brought the light of hope to Lebanon. We condemn the perpetrators of this heinous crime against Lebanon and against the cause of peace in the Middle East..."*

But the words of comfort and support, filtering through the static-muffled speakers, felt very far away – leaders, allies, and mighty armies were on the other side of deserts and oceans... and here I was, once more shivering with cold, uncertainty, and fear, staring at the broken pieces of our little radio, our only connection to the outside world.

What would happen now? What happens to a nation, a town, a family, a child, when the one light of hope in dark blackness is lost?

Bachir Gemayel, Assassinated Lebanese President

chapter 4

It Shall Pass

MY DAD DID NOT EXPRESS MANY OF HIS EMOTIONS in front of us when I was growing up. No matter what happened, I never saw him afraid or depressed or worried or distraught. To show emotion was to show weakness; that was part of our culture anyway, but the war made it so much worse. To be weak meant we would not survive, and for my dad, that was not an option. He wanted us to be strong and tough, so we'd be able to go through the war and survive everything that was happening without being weakened or destroyed by it.

He was a strong man, in more ways than one. I remember his big hands, steady and unshaking, whether he was gripping an automatic weapon or protectively holding us. I remember his back straight and his shoulders squared, braced to stand firm, whatever happened. I remember his broad, smooth brow puckering slightly in the middle, his dark eyebrows pulled close together over his nose in concentration, as he listened for explosions and approaching footsteps. I remember his jaw clenched, his lips set in a straight line of fortitude. And his eyes, piercing, always alert and aware of the shadows in the darkness, the unseen foes. His eyes were deep and understanding, yet he was determined to carefully guard against showing any feeling. He was powerful, undefeatable, unbreakable, and fierce – like a rock, determined to protect us, no matter the cost. And I felt safe and secure in his shelter; nothing could touch me when he was near.

My dad didn't tell us that he loved us – not with his words, anyway. He didn't have the luxury of spending much time laughing, hugging, playing, and listening to us. He had to be on the run constantly; he was either at the farm working, or out guarding and protecting somewhere in the town, so he was away from the house most of the time. Many times he went without food or rest, to ensure we were safe. He had been a soldier as a young man, fighting for his country, and then he transitioned into the role of a soldier who fought solely for his family. That was his primary goal – to protect and provide for us. He was ready to live and die for that cause.

When we were under attack, with bombs falling all around our bunker, we would all be in the corners and under blankets, crying and screaming, but even then my father was so strong. "It's ok, it's ok, we're going to be alright..." he would calmly say to us, trying to soothe our fears. I clutched my head in my hands, trying not to completely fall apart, but thinking, *We're about to die, and you are saying it's ok! It's NOT ok!*

But then I would look up at him. He just stood there so calmly, absorbing all the chaos and tragedy around him, and releasing words of peace and assurance: "You're gonna be ok... we're gonna be fine... Just calm down and pray to God, and he will take care of you. Don't fear... don't be afraid. It's ok... it shall pass..." I remember those words so clearly, because he said them over and over, every time things were terribly wrong: "It shall pass, it shall pass. Trust in God, and it shall pass." That is one of the greatest truths I learned from my dad, and it's what helped me survive and grow: no matter how bad the situation gets, it shall pass. It will not determine the rest of our lives. It might be hard, difficult or stressful, but it will pass.

It has been many years now since I left my parents and their home in Lebanon. I talk to them on the phone, and sometimes see their faces on video chat. And every time I speak with my dad now, he tells me how much he loves me. He wants to make up for all the years that have gone by. He doesn't feel like there is a need any more to be tough and guarded, because he knows that I'm out of danger. I have my own life now, and I live in a different place where I am safe.

But I'm surprised by the way my dad looks. Time has taken a toll on him, and he is old now. His shoulders and back look small and frail, as though the years of carrying the heaviest burdens of life have bent him and slowed him down. His jet black hair is all white now, and lines of pain and concern are etched around his eyes and cheeks, portraying all the stress he absorbed when we were young.

But he has not weakened – I can still see in his eyes a power and strength that transcends this physical body and dying world. He still faithfully cares for my mom, and he spends his days tending his garden of fruit trees. In this way he continues to steadily fill the role of the provider, protector, and sustainer of life in his home.

My dad was, and still is, a great father – kind, loving, generous, caring, forgiving, selfless, honest, compassionate, patient, wise, supportive, determined and loving – and a faithful husband, fearless and brave. He is the man I have looked up to most in all my life.

Mom and Dad Today

chapter 5

A Gang of Brothers

AS KIDS GROWING UP, my brothers and I were like a wolf pack, and other kids in town were intimidated by us. People saw us as five boys who travelled, played, and did everything together. We used our intimidation to our advantage; I always felt like it was a blessing. Nobody could come near me because of my other brothers, and my brothers felt the same way – we had each other's backs.

Joeseph is the oldest, and became the man of the house when Dad was away. He helped Mom take care of us, and was the most responsible of us all. Walid is two years younger than him, but was always the biggest and strongest. Jeel was next, three years younger than Walid, and he was my best friend. We were about the same size and very close in age – I was only one year younger, and I felt like I could talk to him about anything. William is the youngest in the family, almost ten years younger than me, so he wasn't as much a part of our gang until later. But I got to help mom take care of him when he was little, so he has a special place in my heart.

We were definitely close, and loved each other very much. But we were also growing, energetic boys, so inevitably we did not always get along. I remember one year for Christmas, our parents gave us a bike – one bike, for all of us boys to share. Right, like that was really going to work out well! Walid was the one who claimed it. He wouldn't let any of the rest of us ride it, as long as he had it. Joeseph and Jeel sometimes got a turn when he was tired or busy with other things, but I was barely even allowed to come near the thing, most of the time. In fact, Walid even beat me up once or twice when I dared to ask.

One day, I was working outside when I saw Walid stomping towards the garage, dragging the bike along behind him. Somehow he'd gotten a flat tire, and didn't have a pump or patch to fix it. So he put it away and ran off again, to find something else to do. I was devastated, even though I had never been able to ride the bike. It had been enough for me to watch Walid ride it, and hope that someday he would give me a chance. And now the only reason Walid would give me permission to ride it would be because it was useless.

I was watering the garden with my dad's garden hose, absent-mindedly drowning the plants in my preoccupation with the broken bike. Suddenly, the hose in my hand started to look more and more like a bicycle tire tube... I ran over to the abandoned bike and wrenched the flat tire off the wheel, and carried it over to the garden hose. Sure enough, they were almost the same size around! So I used a knife and cut a piece of the hose off and carefully wrapped it around the metal rim of the bicycle wheel, and tied it off.

Then I got on that bike for the first time, and peddled off down the driveway. It actually worked! Ok, so since it wasn't smooth and even, and not exactly the right size, the whole bike wobbled and wiggled like a dog's tail, but I didn't care. I was so proud of myself for fixing it and making it functional again – and now, finally, it was all mine!

It didn't take long to attract the attention of the other kids in the neighborhood, who ran beside me, laughing and cheering for me and my unconventional wheels. It also didn't take long for Walid and my other brothers to notice. I could see them standing around, staring in surprise, and I just grinned at them and waved, but that subtle movement of raising my arm threw off the balance of my shaky ride. I gasped and grabbed both the handle bars again, steadying myself, determined not to fall off in front of them.

"Hey, Abdallah!" Jeel called, "Nice wheels!"

"Yeah, how about giving me a lift!" Joeseph laughed playfully.

"Come over here and share with your brothers!" Walid urged.

"Not a chance!" I shouted back, feeling so liberated and justified after all those months of persecution.

But I couldn't ride very fast, and they easily caught up with me. Joeseph grasped the handlebars, while Walid grabbed me around the waist and hoisted me off. Jeel caught my legs, to keep me from kicking and flailing around in protest, and they held me back while Joeseph got on the seat and managed to pedal in a wavy circle around us. They all cheered for him, over my loud protests and threats. Then they dropped me on the ground and left me behind while they went off and took turns on the bike, pretending to do extreme tricks to impress the girls.

A couple years later, my dad bought a blue Mercedes Benz, and this was the car I learned to drive. When I was ten years old. I wanted so much to drive, and I would sit on the farm tractor, both hands on the big steering wheel, pretending to drive over the hills and valleys surrounding my home. Eventually, Joeseph supervised me as I learned how to actually drive the tractor; he instructed me in what to do, and he stood nearby to keep an eye on me. I practiced and practiced until I felt comfortable on the tractor, and then I asked my dad to teach me how to drive his car. The first few times were really difficult, because driving a tractor was very different from driving a car! The tractor's clutch and gas controls were much harder and stiffer to move, and the car's stick shift was much smoother. It didn't take me too long to adjust, though, and soon I was driving on my own.

My brother, Jeel, was jealous of my newly discovered freedom, so he asked Joeseph and Walid to teach him. He practiced, and had barely got the hang of it, when he decided to steal the car and show off in front of his friends. He drove the car down the hill toward the farms, and took a turn too sharply, hit a rock in the road, and flipped the car on its side. It was a real miracle that he didn't die or get seriously hurt in that crash. But of course, dad was not happy about it; he punished Jeel and forbid him to even touch the *keys* of the car for a long time!

Abdallah and Jeel

chapter 6

The Princess

SHE HAS THE FACE OF AN ANGEL, so sweet with sparkling eyes and a radiant smile; that is my beautiful little sister, Lila. Growing up as the only girl in a family of five brothers, she was wonderfully spoiled, well protected, and deeply loved by all of us – her own personal army of little soldiers.

She would latch on to us boys, because she enjoyed our company and felt safe with us. Sometimes we didn't want to be bothered with her, and we'd say, "No, you can't come to the soccer game – it's boys only! No little girls allowed!" Other times, our parents didn't permit her to go outside, even when we could, and I felt bad that I couldn't take her with us. There was a general perception in our culture that girls were vulnerable and unable to defend themselves, so parents were very protective of their daughters.

When we were inside the bunker, she was my favorite playmate. I would read her stories and she would crack jokes, always doing silly things to cheer us up. Remember that green teddy bear I won at the street carnival? Well, I gave it to her, and she always teased me about it. "This is a boy's teddy bear – not for girls! He looks too manly!" Then she would put dresses on it, to try to make it look more like a girl, and she'd make me have tea parties with her and her dolls, and that poor teddy bear. At first, I resisted, thinking, *I'm too old for this! I will be bored to death!* But then it did provide a distraction, a whimsical fairytale land, where Lila was the princess and I was the honored guest (or faithful servant) at her charming party. I would tell myself to play along, just to amuse her, but inevitably I got sucked in, and ended up really enjoying the chance to escape reality for a while.

Lila at age 6   *Lila Today*

Lila gave me courage and hope, and she was one of my greatest reasons to continue living. I loved her so much that I would remind myself many times not to give up on life, because I couldn't bear the thought of failing her, or letting her down. I also couldn't bear the thought of life without her; her laughter, care, and love were a beautiful light that kept me from being consumed by the darkness.

One day when I was about twelve years old, Lila was playing at a friend's house and I was home alone with my mom, who was very busy, making fresh bread. "Abdallah," Mom said as she kneaded the dough, "please go down to your uncle's house and get some more flour for me." It was such a normal request, and such a simple errand to run.

I left the house and walked down the street toward my uncle's house, passing the house where Lila was playing with her friend, Lina. I heard giggles above my head and looked up to see Lila and Lina on the balcony. Lila looked just like a princess up there, her long black hair fluttering in the breeze, her wide black eyes sparkling as she looked out over her little kingdom.

I continued on down to my uncle's house, and as I returned with the bag of flour, I saw the girls still in their balcony, still giggling and dancing. They saw me this time, so I waved to them. "Hello there, Princess Lila!" I called.

She waved back and leaned over the balcony. "What do you have there, Abdallah? What are you taking home to Mom?"

"Gold, your highness! I'm bringing bags of gold to the queen mother!" They giggled as I dramatically lifted the bag of flour, and then they went back to their game.

As I neared our house, I heard the familiar *BOOM* of bombs in the distance. I immediately dropped the bag of flour on the street and ran as fast as I could. Just as I came into the kitchen, there was a sudden and powerful *WHOOSH!* The whole house shook and the glass shattered everywhere. Mom grabbed me and ran to the bathroom to hide. In the bathroom we could hear the explosions continue. Mom crouched on the floor and held me close, her blouse covered with flour, and her hands still sticky from her work. I breathed deeply and was comforted by the familiar smell of her, of her kitchen, of our home.

"She's dead, she's dead, I know she must be dead..." my mom began to mutter to herself. Then my heart stopped because I knew she was thinking of Lila. The mutters became more panicked and desperate, getting louder and louder until they were screams, choked by sobs that wracked her whole body. "My baby! My Lila! Oh God, my sweet baby girl!" She continued to hold me, to squeeze me close as she wailed, her broken heart bleeding out through her tears. "My daughter! She's dead, I know she is...!" Her body trembled and I was terrified and frozen.

The balcony... all I could see was that balcony, and my beautiful sister waving and giggling. That explosion was so close – you don't have to be a military expert to understand that when you feel the pressure and your whole body quakes with the impact, it had landed incredibly close. And it wasn't just one; the sound of explosions kept coming, some very near and some further away. A tiny, rational piece of me knew that I had to wait to go outside and find my sister until the attack was over, so I tried to wait. I waited for about ten minutes, and they were the longest ten minutes of my life. But with each minute that passed, each *BOOM* that hit, my mom became more wild – I was watching her go crazy with grief and despair. My last memory of Lila on the balcony twisted and boiled into a nightmare of blood and mutilation that I could not stop. I held my head in my hands and squeezed my eyes shut, begging the images to disappear, but the explosions and my mom's terror only intensified them.

"I want to go check on my sister!" I pleaded, my voice muffled in Mom's chest, where she held me tight.

"No, no," she cried, "It's too dangerous! We must wait..."

But I couldn't wait any more. The thoughts and images of Lila's mangled body tormented me beyond what I could bear. So I wrenched away from my mom and ran as fast as I could from the house. I had to find Lila and bring her home, even if I was killed in the process. I did not feel like a brave soldier without my brothers, the rest of Lila's royal guard, but I was desperate. I ran into the street and strained to see the house with the balcony. Only, there was no balcony anymore – it was crumbled and twisted in a pile of rubble on the ground, in a huge black hole. The front door was also gone, broken apart on the ground, among shards of glass and rocks. Destruction was everywhere. I stared in horror at the scene and my legs trembled. I was too shocked to move or respond, and was barely aware of the bombs that continued to fall all over our town.

Lila is dead. My thoughts declared in a hollow tone that echoed through my empty heart. *Should I go down there and find the pieces of my sister? Should I go back home?* Both options terrified me. How could I possibly see my sister's body, broken and bleeding, buried under mounds of rubble? How could I possibly go back to my mom and be the one to confirm her worst nightmare? *What should I do? What do I DO now?*

The shaking in my limbs turned to fire that ignited me into action, and without really knowing what I was doing, I ran toward the mangled balcony. I had to find Lila myself. I couldn't leave this task for my mom to do alone. I had to be brave.

I carefully walked through the rubble, looking for an arm, a leg, a scrap of her clothing, a clump of her hair, anything that I could identify as a piece of a human being... a piece of my sister. Then I heard shouts through the broken window, from inside the battered house. "We're all well! We're all well! Go back home!" It was a male voice, Lina's father. "We're all well," he assured me again, "but please just go back home now! Don't stand outside like that – it's not safe!"

I didn't believe him - I couldn't believe him. I stumbled over rocks and glass through the gaping mouth where the door once was. "Where is she?"

I demanded. The room was dark and dust was so thick in the air that I couldn't see anything. I squinted and rubbed my eyes, and realized that I had been crying. My nose was runny and my whole face was swollen, I was gasping and choking on smoke and fear. I could not make myself believe she was alive, no matter how many times he said it. He was just telling me this because he wanted me to be safe; he was trying to get me to go home before I was killed. I knew he couldn't be telling me the truth, so I kept moving forward blindly in the room, following the sound of the voice that pleaded with me to go home.

"Abdallah, I'm here!" The sound of Lila's small, frightened voice sparked relief in my heart: it seemed so *alive* – I didn't think I would ever hear it again. In a moment we were in each other's arms, and my heart was full. *She's alive! My sister is alive! Thank you, Jesus, oh thank you!*

In the midst of our joyful reunion, Lina's father urged me to stay with them in the house until the attack ended. But my thoughts quickly shifted from my sister to my mom, who by this time surely believed I was dead, too. "No no, I can't stay. I have to tell Mom that Lila is alive and safe!"

At that moment, I heard my mom outside of the house, stumbling over the rocks and trying to find a way inside. She was wailing and screaming, loudly and passionately mourning the daughter she thought was dead. I grabbed Lila's hand and ran to the entrance with her – I knew Mom wouldn't believe me if I came alone. "Lila is alive!" I called weakly, my own voice choked with emotion. "She was safe inside the house," I said, trying to console her with news that seemed too good to be true. She collapsed on the ground, and couldn't believe her eyes.

Mom reached out for Lila, grabbed her tightly and held her close. The three of us ran home together, even as missiles continued to rain down on our town in the distance. Mom kept touching Lila's head and hair, checking everything about her, just to reassure herself that her baby really was safe and unharmed. She continued to weep, but I could tell that her panicked sobs of despair were slowly becoming tears of relief and release.

The air raid ended, and as silence descended on our home, my mom used her apron to dab her eyes and nose. "I'm sorry, Abdallah," she said wearily. "I don't want this life for you. I want you to have so much more... I want you to be safe and free and happy... and I feel so helpless, because I want it for you so much, but I cannot give it to you... a mother should be able to protect her children, and I just can't... Oh, Abdallah, I love you and your brothers and sister so much."

I didn't know what to say, or how to comfort her. That day I got a glimpse of how heavy a burden my mom carried – the weight of the whole war, and the future of her children. She suffered more than I ever knew, but she was so brave and strong in the midst of it. She fought her own battles with weapons of fierce love and care for us.

chapter 7

Playing at War

SOMETIMES, WHEN ALL WAS QUIET AND CALM OUTSIDE the bunker, our mom would say, "You can go outside and play!" That magic phrase was like a key, unlocking a cage. My brothers and I cheered and jumped up and down, dancing around our mom, like freed birds flapping our wings: "Are you really saying this? Am I really hearing this? I can go and play now?"

I barely noticed the strained, concerned expression on her face, as she held my oldest brother by the shoulders and made him look at her and focus. "Ten minutes, Joeseph!" she emphasized, "You've got ten minutes to go outside and play, and then come right back inside."

"Yes, Mom," my brother impatiently nodded as the rest of us ran for the bunker door.

"Do not go past the driveway! Stay close to your dad's car. I am going to the house with Lila to do some cooking. If you hear me call for you, you must make your brothers come right away. You understand? Do not leave any of them behind. Don't take your eyes off them. Remember, only ten minutes!"

"Yes, Mom!" Joeseph said over his shoulder as he pulled away from her and ran after us, out into the sunshine.

Sunshine! Fresh air! What a perfect day to be outside and play! I took a deep breath in, and couldn't help but laugh as I exhaled. Never mind the acrid stench of war that hung in the air, never mind the debris that cluttered the street or the rubble that was left from so many houses in our neighborhood. For everything that was wrong in my world, I had somehow won ten minutes of freedom to just be a little boy. These were my favorite times - we kids could go outside and play, releasing the weight of all the stress and hurt we lived under every day.

My mom at 20

The four of us played as often as we could outside, in the garden around our house. Our favorite game to play together, ironically, was War, imitating the soldiers and fighters that we saw, with all the drama and fun our imaginations could provide. We would divide into two "armies" – always Joeseph and I on one side, and Jeel and Walid in the other. We built forts for ourselves out of anything we could find – sandbags, cardboard, old chairs, or sheets of metal. Then we'd throw rocks and fire crackers at each other. The intention, of course, was never to actually hit each other, but to distract our "enemies" and destroy their fort. But it was inevitable that we had accidents - like the time I hit one of my brothers squarely in the back of the head with a sharp rock, or like the time I didn't throw a firecracker fast enough and it blew up in my hand.

We even found some old rocket launchers that the army had thrown away because they didn't work right any more. We had so much fun, putting these big cylinders on our shoulders, and packing them with firecrackers to shoot at each other. The sound it made was tremendous, shaking us to our very bones!

Those weren't the only dangerous toys we played with, either. There were these knives that soldiers used to attach to the front of their machine guns, like bayonets, and we would collect them and make sheaths for them that we could tie to our thighs. One day, Walid was showing off how fast he could pull the knife out and slip it back in its sheath, kind of like he was a Wild West sharpshooter. With wide-eyed amazement, we all watched as, with a flash, he yanked it out and jammed it back in, once, then twice, then- with a shocked and terrible scream, Walid looked down at the knife, which was buried to the hilt in his leg.

Another time, we were playing hide-and-seek, and Jeel was running away from me. I tried to catch up with him, but I couldn't, so I figured that tripping him would be my best chance. I stretched out and kicked at the back of his leg. It made him trip, and when he fell, his hand landed on an old, rusty, forgotten Spam can that was half buried in the dirt. I was so afraid as I ran to the house to tell my mom, just knowing that when my dad got home from work and learned what I had caused, he would punish me. Mom ran outside and she wrapped Jeel's hand in a towel, and he had almost passed out from all the pain and blood. The cut was about six inches wide and two inches deep. He had to get 25 stitches in his hand that day. When we played War, we didn't mess around!

We also liked to play at the public school playground, which was within walking distance from our house. The school had given up on locking gates or putting signs up to keep people out, so it sort of became a public park, though not a particularly safe one. We had 24/7 access to it, and so it became rather lawless. It was a concrete slab that always glittered with broken glass, which crunched under our feet. Of course, for boys who played rough, the glass caused a lot of problems over the years: scrapes, cuts, and sometimes worse. One time, while playing soccer, my team was losing and my brothers were winning. I hated to lose, and out of anger and frustration, I tripped Jeel, and he fell onto some shards of glass, and a big piece dug deep into his thigh.

We met up with other neighborhood boys there, and usually our favorite game to play was soccer. But sometimes the school would be abandoned for months, so we would go inside the building to play Hide-and-Seek or War. We used the desks to build elaborate forts, and had fun being reckless and wild in our own unsupervised world – which was, ironically, in a school building, in the middle of a real-life war zone.

I remember one day when our mom allowed us a few minutes to play in the front yard. My brothers climbed onto the hood of our dad's car, a 1965 BMW, and we were all talking at once about what we could play: Tag? Soldiers? Walid took charge and declared Hide-and-Seek as the game of the day. Joeseph glanced uneasily at the house, remembering Mom's instructions for him to watch us carefully. "I'm not sure that's a good-" he started to say, but Walid rolled his eyes and said, "Oh come on! It's not like we have many places to hide in this little area. Behind the car, under the car, in the car..."

"Hey, don't give away all our good hiding places!" Jeel teased, and we laughed again. "Our time is running out. Let's just play! Walid, it was your idea, so you're 'it'!"

Before Joeseph could form a good argument or a better idea, Walid jumped off the car, squatted on the ground, covered his face with his hands and began to count: "One!... Two!... Three!..."

Jeel and I smothered our giggles and ran around the side of the car. He quietly opened the door and folded the driver's seat forward; then he pointed to me, and pointed inside, behind the driver's seat. I nodded that I understood, and climbed inside to huddle close behind the seat. As I did, I saw Joeseph running to a mound of rubble beside the bunker, just as eager as the rest of us to join the game.

"Four!... Five!..." Walid kept counting, and Jeel reached in to fold the seat back up again, preparing to dash to his own hiding place.

"Six!... Sev-" Walid stopped short, suddenly aware of a faint but ominous deep sound: *boom.* We all froze, Jeel still holding the car door open and looking out in the distance. A second later, the sound came again, but this time closer and louder: *BOOM.* A missile attack.

"Boys! Run inside! Run inside!" We heard our mom scream at the open door of the house, but we were already running to her. The car was still open, the seat was still folded down, but the game was forgotten. In our world, hiding was not for fun, it was for survival. I got there first, then Walid, then Jeel. Joeseph was close behind, but not close enough. "Come on, my Jo-!" Mom stood at the door, reaching her arms out for him, but her call was drowned out by a heavy explosion. I could feel the force and the heat of it as it landed on the car – the car that only seconds ago was our playground.

Joeseph stumbled from the impact only inches from my mom, and the vacuum of the explosion pulled him back. Mom took a large step forward, holding the doorframe with one hand, and grabbing Joeseph's shirt with the other. She yanked him inside, slamming the door shut.

More bombs were falling all around our house, and we were stunned with terror, but Mom didn't hesitate. She had become a military expert, a super-soldier, out of necessity and passion to protect her family. She herded us all into the bathroom in the middle of the house, where we crouched together and waited.

That's when we saw the blood all over Joeseph's face, all over Mom's hands and arms from where she had grabbed and held him. A piece of shrapnel from the car had hit him in the back of the head and he was bleeding terribly. We couldn't go to the hospital – we couldn't go anywhere, and we didn't know how long the attack would last. What if Joeseph bled to death before we could get help? He was already going into shock, and he looked pale and clammy.

Lila whimpered, and Jeel held her and rocked her, which seemed to comfort them both. Mom grabbed towels and worked hard to stop the bleeding. As she gently cleaned his face, Walid whispered, "Is he going to... die?" I shuddered, because it was what we were all thinking, but were afraid to ask. "No," Mom replied, without looking away from Joeseph, without slowing her work. Tears were filling her eyes, but she refused to let them fall. "No, he will not die..."

All the while, the bombs were landing all around our house... one after another, after another, after another. They shook the walls and shattered the windows, and pounded the cruel reality of my world into my mind. *BOOM - Foolish boy! BOOM – You think you have the right to go outside for fun? BOOM – Your life is War, not Play! BOOM, BOOM – You don't deserve joy! You will never be free!* **BOOM** *– There is no hope for you!*

Twenty minutes passed like this, but it seemed like hours to me.

Meanwhile, my dad was 30 miles away, working in the wheat fields.

The fields were wide open, and he could see our town on top of the hill from there. That day, he knew a missile had landed very close to the house – he could see the smoke from the burning car. He was so afraid, he dropped everything right away and drove his work car home to check on us, wondering all the time if we had survived. When he got home, we were still hiding in the bathroom.

"Nadya! Joeseph! Walid! Abdallah!" he called, frantically searching for us all. When I heard his voice, I ran to him, and told him about Joeseph. My parents put Joeseph in Dad's work car and drove him to the Red Cross station, which was in the next town, about 25 minutes away.

"Please Dad, can I go too?" I begged.

"No, I'm sorry, but it is not safe," he told me. "We need you to stay home with the others."

The doctors were able to remove the shrapnel from Joeseph's head, and he came home with a lot of stitches. It took him a few weeks to recover, and he couldn't play much with us. We had to be very careful with him, so his wounds wouldn't reopen. Every time I looked at his stitches, fear gripped me. His pain reminded me that the threat was real – I could have lost my brother, and I could lose my own life, at any time.

chapter 8

Lessons Learned

WHEN WE WERE LITTLE, we attended the public school near our house. On calm days, we would wake up early and get ready, then we would walk to the school, only about ten minutes away, all the while wondering if the school would even be open that day. It was a tall building with windows that made up the majority of one side. I don't remember much about my education at the school, because I was very young, and because there were so many other traumatic memories filling my childhood. But I do remember history class...

Lebanese history is significant, and is much older than U.S. history, or even European history. Its earliest accounts date back as far as 3000 B.C. In class, the teacher would lecture about the culture and sophistication of our civilization as it evolved through ancient and classical eras. Then the teacher would tell us about warriors, conquerors, and heroes, and I wondered, *Why are we learning about a bunch of old, dead guys? What does any of this have to do with me? I need to learn things that can really help me now.* I'm sure this is a sentiment that many kids have when it comes to history classes. It wasn't until years later that I realized the value of those lessons.

From 1516-1918, Lebanon was under the power of the Turkish Ottoman Empire; that's four hundred years of outside forces having power and authority in our land! That regime finally ended when the Lebanese people rose up and fought back, with the help of allies, for their liberation. And less than one century later, I was living in a piece of history that seemed to be repeating itself – outside forces were once again vying for the control and power over my homeland and my people. I knew we needed to look back into our history, and learn from the errors and victories of our ancestors; we must study our past if we are to have any hope for our future.

Often, I would walk to school as a child, only to find that many of the windows on the front of the huge, five-story building were shattered again. It looked as though a giant had punched it in the face and knocked out its teeth – and essentially, that is what the war was doing to my education. My shoes crunched over the broken glass in the yard, and I saw a janitor sweeping up some rubble and shards around the entrance, doing his best to make this a safe place for children again. On the front door was a sign: "CLOSED: No school today." Our education was shattered like the glass.

The public school education was okay, but my parents had a higher standard for our learning. For example, that school taught French as a foreign language, and my parents thought it would be more useful for us to learn English. So, when I was in fifth grade, we all transferred to a private school about fifteen minutes away. It was expensive, but my parents felt it was worth the cost to give us a better education.

My dad would drive us to school in his old BMW, and we were all so embarrassed. It was such an ugly old clunker, and we didn't want our friends to see us in it.

"No no, dad, just drop us off here!" we would beg, while we were still out of sight of the school yard.

"Nonsense, I can take you all the way to the front door!" my dad would say, ignoring our pleas and protests and groans.

After school, my brothers and I would rush out of the building and down the street, to try to meet him on the road before he arrived at the front door. I'm ashamed to say it wasn't just the car that embarrassed me back then; my dad worked hard at the farm to provide for our family, but he would come to our school in his shabby farm work clothes. I wished he would wear a suit and tie all the time, just so my friends would be impressed. Little did I realize then all the sacrifices my dad made, just because he loved us and wanted the best for us.

"Photosynthesis is the process used by plants to create energy. Sunlight and carbon dioxide are absorbed by the leaves, and water is absorbed by the roots. The sun, gas, and water do not destroy the plants – together, they give life to the plants. Then plants create glucose and release oxygen into the air, which gives life to us all." Mr. Isaa, my ninth grade biology teacher, was trying to explain the day's lesson to us as clearly as possible, but also as quickly as possible. He knew that any minute, he could be interrupted by the wailing siren that would alert us to yet another barrage of Katyusha missiles. Every moment of instruction was precious.

This time was precious to me, too. As Mr. Isaa outlined the steps in the process of photosynthesis on the blackboard, I sketched leaves in my notebook – healthy, beautiful leaves, that received life and gave life freely and generously, like a wealthy benefactor or a noble ruler.

"So, first, we have carbon dioxide – that is CO_2 – that enters the stomata..."

I drew veins and texture on the leaves and wondered what my town, my country, my world would be like if there were no missiles or machine guns, no need for tanks or bunkers... if the priority was to give life, rather than take life.

"Next, we have water – that is H_2O – that enters the roots..."

How much stronger and happier and healthier would we all be? I couldn't even imagine what that would feel like... to be like the leaves. To be free to live, and in doing so, bring life to others.

"Then, we have the sunlight-"

The teacher's explanation was drowned out by a piercing sound, an alarm, so loud that at first we couldn't hear the explosions getting closer and closer. Mr. Isaa paused at the blackboard for only a second before he tossed the piece of chalk in helpless resignation, and turned around to face us, no longer a biology teacher in a classroom, but a civilian defender in a war zone. "Ok, everybody please follow me quickly, but do not panic..." He led us out into the hallway, where the principal was hastening all of us to the stairs. We were on the second floor, and we had only enough time to get to the first floor and take shelter in the long, inside hallways until the attack passed.

After the alarm stopped, the school closed for the rest of the day. It was only 10:30 on Monday morning, but they did not want to risk the lives of so many students. The danger of rockets and mortar was still near, so we were hurried out of the school, loaded into armored military personnel carriers, and driven home.

The next day when I got to my classroom, the door was closed and locked, and there was a sign on it that said: "Mr. Isaa's Biology class has been moved to the first floor." I peered through the little window on the door, and saw that the large windows on the far wall were gone, and the desks and books were all over the room, broken to pieces and half burned to ashes. The blackboard was smashed, but the lesson about photosynthesis was still there - a large crack had broken apart the crude chalk drawing of the sun. It seemed strange that only yesterday morning, this was where I sat with my friends and recited the process of photosynthesis.

It seemed even more strange that after all this destruction, the class was simply moved down the hall, and life was expected to go on. But one of the biggest lessons I learned in school was how to improvise. If one room was destroyed, we used another; if one route to school was blocked, we found another. This was life – like the plants that somehow grew up out of rocks, sand, and ash, we learned how to survive and keep living, no matter what happened.

I sat in the new classroom that day, with my books open and my pencil in hand, staring hard at the words the teacher was writing on the board. I desperately wanted to concentrate and learn whatever I could – even if it was just a few words or equations. I wanted to learn about something that would bring me life.

These valuable moments in school were my chance to feel normal, to fight for some hope for my future. I wanted to be just like other kids, other students. But while students in other parts of the world were probably tapping their fingers and watching the clock, eagerly anticipating the bell for the end of class, for lunch, for recess, or for the end of the day, I braced myself for the very probable sound of the alarm, warning us at any moment to take cover. When would the next bomb fall? Where would it be? Would it hit the school? Would I have a house to go home to? Some days, I held that tension in my chest and neck all day long, and there would be no alarm. Every once in a while, we got to stay in school all day. But it only made the anxiety worse the next day – the likelihood of an attack was that much greater, so it was that much harder to focus on academics.

Then the alarm would go off again. We might have been able to spend two normal days in school before it happened. And while students in other parts of the world jumped on school buses, we were taken home in armored cars once more.

The next day, I gathered my books and headed to the school again, trying to pretend to have a chance at a normal education. But when I arrived outside, I looked up at the space where my classroom was yesterday, and the brick was crumbled, the windows shattered. They would have to move Biology class again, but where? How many rooms were still functional? Many of the open gaps from the broken windows of Monday were now covered up with cheap plywood or plastic sheets. I came through the yard and near the front doors, but they were closed and chained shut, and a sign was posted: "CLOSED - There is no school today."

So I turned around to walk back to the safety of the bunker. On the way, I met some of my classmates and told them the school was closed. While other students in other parts of the world probably would cheer at the news that they had no school, we hung our heads in disappointment and trudged home. "Maybe I'll see you tomorrow..." we would say to each other, but we knew the school would probably be closed for days or weeks. And even when it did open, our parents may or may not allow us to return, depending on the risks.

As much as we wanted to, as much we tried, we knew we were not like other students.

I would say that all this time away from school gave me plenty of time to study and do my homework, but the distractions were so great, and survival was more important. The priority was always just to make it through another day. I would try to learn and better myself, try to read my books by candlelight in the bunker, but the angry and painful shouts, the sounds of bombs and machine guns, made me crazy. I slammed my book shut and shouted to no one in particular: "You know what? This school thing is not working. It's not for people like us. We are living in a war zone! So why should I bother anymore?"

But despite all the obstacles, I was able to continue through the years – improvising, surviving, and moving forward, and I earned my high school diploma. It wasn't the best system and certainly wasn't the best situation, but I didn't let that stop me from getting an education. I didn't let it stop me from fighting to learn.

chapter 9

Handling Weapons—I'm Dead!

I WAS BORN IN WAR and lived most of my life in war. I don't remember much of the early years of my life, but one of my earliest memories was when I was about 7 years old, and I started recognizing and making more sense of things that I saw and heard... things like gunfire and the sound of explosions.

In my parents' house, we had almost every kind of machine gun. We had M16s, AKs and grenades, all right there inside the house. And they weren't even kept in a safe or a box; no, my father wanted to have them handy, right where he could reach them at a moment's notice. "You see, Son," he explained to me, "if someone breaks into the house and tries to kill us, I don't have time to scramble around and unlock a cabinet to get a weapon out. I need to be able to defend you very quickly."

So we developed an awareness of what was dangerous at a very early age. Even though grenades were within reach and looked like tempting toys, with their small round shape, their bumpy texture, and their shiny pins, I knew they were a "No, no!" and my hands would be smacked harshly if I even reached out for one as a baby. As I got older, grenades were so common and familiar that I could just pick one up and carry it around like a lemon, in a room where six or seven people were sitting, and nobody would say or do anything about it.

The kids in my town grew up fast. We didn't have time to be immature and irresponsible, to sit around and wait for the years to tell us we were adults. We had to learn how to defend and protect ourselves, to be prepared for extreme situations – to carry and shoot a gun. I've heard about kids in other parts of the world who foolishly play with guns and shoot themselves or someone else because they don't know any better. But we never had problems like that. Even though weapons surrounded us in our homes and in the streets, we knew the dangers and we knew how to handle them. We didn't mess with them unless we had to use them against somebody who was trying to kill us.

My oldest brother, Joeseph, taught me how to shoot a gun when I was eight years old. "I want to learn how to shoot," I told him, and very casually he said, "Ok yeah, no problem, I'll show you." He carried a hunting gun and I followed him out to a field. He demonstrated by shooting a few birds, and he made it look so easy and effortless that I eagerly reached for the gun. "I'm going to shoot the next bird, not you!" He raised his eyebrows at my confidence and handed the gun to me. It was heavier than I imagined, but I wanted to prove myself to my brother. Then Joeseph turned his back to me, and bent down, gathering and counting his birds.

I hoisted the gun up with both hands, and put the butt of the gun right in front of my nose. I squinted cross-eyed through the lens, scanning the sky for my prey. Then I saw him – an unassuming little bird that fluttered into my view, and then landed happily on a bush nearby. I smiled to myself, *That bird is making this so easy!* I could already envision the poof of feathers from my perfect shot, as I gripped the gun tightly and squeezed the trigger.

POW! All of a sudden, the whole universe was spinning out of control. My brain shook, my eyes pounded, and I couldn't see. *What was that?!* I panicked and screamed, scared to death that somehow I had killed myself or blown my face off. *That wasn't supposed to happen! Why did the gun do that to me?!*

When Joeseph first saw that I basically punched myself in the face with the gun, he started laughing, thinking it was really funny, and I was just being a stupid little brother. But then he heard my screams and saw that I had a black eye and that my face was swelling up to the size of a pumpkin, and he ran to me, yelling, "What's wrong? What happened?"

The pain was horrible; I felt like a boxer who was losing in the twelfth round of a match, all bruised and dazed. Through my tears and hyperventilating gasps, I bawled, "I'm gonna... tell Dad! This is... all your fault! You... didn't teach me... you didn't... help me!"

Joeseph knew I was right. He moaned, "That's it, Dad is going to *kill* me!" Then he lost it, jumping up and down, screaming in fear and panic. He was so scared to go home that night, knowing that he would surely be punished, and that he deserved it. He never made that mistake again.

My dad taught me and my brothers how to use a machine gun. He had an M16 in the house, and he knew he had to teach us at an early age, so we could defend ourselves. Before we were even allowed to talk about shooting it, he showed us how to handle it in a safe way. "You must respect the weapon," Dad taught us. "It is no joke! It is not a toy. It can kill you and kill others. You have to be very careful when you hold it and carry it." He made us practice checking the chamber multiple times to ensure that it was empty before we handled it. Then he taught us how to clean it, so it would always work properly.

Dad was much more thorough than Joeseph when he taught me to shoot. He stood next to me with the gun and told me each step as he demonstrated: "You put the gun here on your shoulder, and hold very still. Take the safety off, breathe out, hold your breath... Aim... and fire!" I flinched at the loud and echoing *BANG!* and then I watched my dad lower the smoking gun from his shoulder. "Then you make sure the chamber is clear," he continued, "and put the safety back on." Then he helped me place the gun securely on my shoulder and slowly talked me through the steps again.

My dad and the other men in his generation were formally trained soldiers in the Lebanese Armed Forces, the 4th Infantry Brigade. After that division was disbanded in 1983, the men came home with most of the weapons and equipment, which is why we had such an extensive arsenal in our bunker. They also used their military training and experience to form a militia in our town – not to be aligned with any religious or political group, but to give our community the chance to defend and protect ourselves. They set up military checkpoints around town, with guards who inspected people coming in and out of town, to ensure they were not there to harm us. One of these checkpoints was not too far from our house, and people like my dad and my uncle and our neighbors took turns standing guard at this post. I remember going there to play in this secure vicinity as a child. I thought of it as a "cool spot to hang out." My friends and I could touch the machine guns and pretend to be soldiers. We weren't told to go home, because we got to be a part of the community in this special way.

When he was old enough, Joe joined the militia. I would hang around him at the post, and when he needed a restroom break, he would let me stand guard in his place at the checkpoint for a few minutes. He gained a lot of knowledge about the weapons, so he showed me how to throw grenades and fire launchers under his cautious supervision. Then he let me practice using bigger machine guns - the ones they put on tanks. I had fun with those, aiming at abandoned buildings and finding other harmless targets to practice on. Joe also taught me military skills and strategies, like how to set an ambush.

It's hard to believe all the dangerous things we tried and practiced with no adult supervision, nobody watching or questioning or stopping us. Looking back now, I think there were many things I probably shouldn't have done; but then, I'm glad that I did. Those experiences gave me the knowledge and wisdom I have today, and gave me a different perspective on things like conflict, violence, protection, and peace.

When I turned 14 years old, I became part of the militia, too. I used to stay on guard at our post or go on patrols around town with other people of all ages. Many nights I stood watch, anxiously waiting to face anyone who threatened my home and my family. I was terrified, but I put on a brave face... I could not let the enemy believe I was afraid of them.

Even with all the guns and grenades that surrounded me, I was seriously lacking in my supply of hope. I had seen too many terrible things happen, and there were too many terrible possibilities ahead, for me to see any glimmer of light in that darkness. But I have learned that hope is the greatest weapon any of us can have in this life. It had been captured by our enemies, and somehow I needed to launch a counter-attack to reclaim it.

chapter 10

Becoming the Fighter

A KARATE DOJO OPENED NEAR OUR HOUSE when I was young. It was unique in our town - something new and different. It was a breath of fresh air to the community, to have something arrive that wasn't terrible, something that provided kids with opportunities to make us better people; we just didn't have places like that in our town. The instructor's name was Simon, and he came from Beirut. We thought of him as sort of a hero, because he was courageous enough to do this, and he was an excellent instructor.

My parents enrolled Jeel and I in karate classes, to give us something else to focus on besides the war. Even with all the things that threatened our joy, my parents were still hopeful that things would change, that the war would come to an end, and that we would have a better future than what they lived through. They always fought for hope, and that was something I didn't understand back then; with everything that was happening, it seemed like they shouldn't believe there would be a better day.

We went to the dojo four days a week, and it was a stress reliever for us. We enjoyed it so much, because it gave us an outlet to vent. One of the drills the instructor had us do involved brooms. Now, brooms in Lebanon were different – not plastic or soft, flexible materials; they were made completely of straw, straight and sharp and thick. We were instructed to make a fist and punch the end of the brooms, to make our knuckles stronger. When I think of it now, it seems strange that he made little kids do that; surely there are better and safer ways to do this, but we didn't know any better. I don't know if this exercise really strengthened our hands, but it did bruise our knuckles. We weren't required to hit the broom very hard, but because of the anger, frustration, rage, and violence we lived in, we started punching hard, taking all the anger inside of us and releasing it without restraint on the brooms. I punched until my knuckles bled, and my bones almost showed through.

That's how my martial arts journey started.

Karate was not my first exposure to fighting. My uncle was a well-known wrestler, and when I was a little kid, maybe three or four years old, he started to train me and my brothers. He saw potential in me, so he focused special attention on training me. He had us compete within our family, so we would team up – Joseph and I, and Jeel and Walid.

We also had a lot of extended family overseas in Bolivia, and when they came to visit us in Lebanon, they would arrange tournaments for us kids to wrestle each other, and they bet money on us. They enjoyed wrestling so much, and wrestling was huge in my family's history.

In one of these tournaments, Walid and I were in a final match together, and he chose to use a wrestling move called a "piledriver" on me that he knew would help him win, but it almost broke my back in half. He put my head between his legs and lifted my legs up and dropped me on my head. I got the wind knocked out of me. I couldn't breathe, and it took me a few minutes to figure out what was going on around me. It shocked my whole system, and I was terrified that I would be paralyzed. But I didn't want to show how badly I was injured, because everybody was sitting around and watching and cheering. I tried to suck it up and be a man about it and not show any signs of weakness, but I was just a little kid, about five years old. Fortunately, my dad realized how badly I was hurt, and he ran to me and told me not to move. He was so mad at my brother for doing that, but it happened so fast, he didn't have the chance to tell him not to do it.

From that moment on, my dad told us boys, "I don't want you to wrestle." Most of it was just fun, we used moves that we knew wouldn't hurt us, but once we started doing stupid things, we had the potential to cause serious harm. My dad knew we were taking it too far, so the family stopped having the fights. I remember hearing him tell my uncle, "This is the end of it! I don't want my kids to do this stuff anymore. I don't want any of them to get hurt."

But I kept secretly training, and I got better and better at wrestling. My brothers and I would wrestle each other at home while my dad was out of the house at the farm, almost every day. My mom would be so upset with us, screaming at us, "Stop! Don't do this!" But we would slam the bedroom door and lock her out. She would stand there and bang on the door, commanding us to stop, but we wouldn't listen to her.

I learned and practiced karate for five years, and I became a great fighter, earning my black belt and winning many competitions. But after five years, the dojo closed and Simon moved away. I respected him as a leader and teacher, because he molded our self-esteem and confidence and helped us become better people. This is the beauty of martial arts: from deep down, it changes you into a different human being – one that is very respectful and very humble.

As I got older, my parents moved me to a different gym where I learned Taekwondo, which I practiced for almost ten years. I competed many times, but one match stands out the most because of the dramatic way the whole thing went down.

My instructor came to me and he said, "We have a tournament coming up, and I would like for you to go with us and compete."

I'd been going to the classes for less than six months and only had my yellow belt at that time. I said, "But I'm just a newbie, fresh into Taekwondo. Will they even let me compete?"

He just shrugged without a hint of concern and said, "Don't worry, we'll put a different belt on you, so you can compete with higher ranks."

That was not the response I expected! I said, "But what if they're too good and beat me up?"

He smiled and patted me on the shoulder reassuringly. "Don't worry about it! I know you so well, you're gonna be fine. Trust me, you'll be just fine."

His words did little to comfort me. I was a beginner, and everyone who was competing in the tournament had higher ranks. I felt like they had so much advantage over me, because they had all the skills, all the knowledge – and all I had were doubts and concerns. I was hesitant and fearful that it would not go the way I wanted, and I believed I would be defeated and humiliated. But my instructor trusted that I would be fine. I wondered, "Where is he getting all this confidence from?"

In training at the gym, we would spar, and every time I sparred with my instructor, I would hold back, out of respect. I didn't want to be too aggressive or show off, because I knew he could really beat me up and take me out, if he wanted to. But sometimes, I would test my limits, sneaking in some clever moves, just to show him, "I'm here, and you can't just walk all over me!" Sometimes I took it to the next level with him, so he knew I was good. That's why he knew what I was capable of, and that I could handle the tournament.

The time for the match came, and I walked out on the mat with all the gear on. The opponent was bigger than me, with big muscles and an intimidating presence. As I sized him up, I thought, "Man, this guy is gonna destroy me. I don't stand a chance!"

Then he started spinning and jumping in the air, doing all kinds of crazy moves. I was hesitant and concerned, but I never backed down when it came to fighting. So I decided, "You know what, I'm just gonna let him do his thing, and see how I can counter with one big shot, and that will be it, that should do it for me. I'm not gonna be spinning, jumping, or anything like that. I'm gonna avoid everything he does. I'm just gonna hit him once, that's it. If it works, I'll be fine. But if it doesn't work, this guy will surely beat me."

I blocked a few of his kicks and punches. And then he did this move called "the spinning back-kick": he spun his whole body around and brought his leg up high. I moved back, and as his leg came back down, I came up with a roundhouse kick to his head. My opponent fell back on the mat, knocked out cold.

I stood there for a moment, unsure of what just happened. I couldn't believe my eyes, and asked myself, "Did I just knock that guy out?" Then pride welled up in me as I realized that my plan worked! I was so happy, so proud, and my team started jumping up and down and cheering for me. But we went from being joyful and celebrating, to all of a sudden sinking into deep concern because he was not moving.

I thought he would get up and jump right back in, but he didn't. The medics on the sidelines rushed forward and started working on him, because he was unconscious. It was terrifying to witness. I hit him so hard that it shook his brain, and it took about ten minutes to wake him up. I heard my coach say quietly to me, "If he didn't have that headgear on, this strike would have killed him."

When he did wake up, he wanted to continue fighting. He got up and started looking for me, and the referee waved his hands and shook his head, shouting, "It's over! You got knocked down!" But the opponent wouldn't accept it. He turned the whole thing into a big scene. "No, I didn't lose! How could I lose?"

In the meantime, my team was rejoicing, and I got a gold medal for the fight. Finally, once he calmed down, my opponent came to me with a smile on his face and gave me a huge hug. He said, "You're the man! I can't believe you did that, I have so much respect for you! Nobody has knocked me out before." As I received his compliment, I was thinking, "You probably don't know, but I'm not even at your same level!" But I didn't say anything about that to him. Instead, I thanked him, and we became close friends after that.

After my time in Taekwondo, I switched to kickboxing at the same gym. And when I moved to the United States, I did Thai boxing for many years. I got certified to become an instructor under the Thai boxing association.

Also I studied jujitsu, which is Brazilian martial arts. I'm currently working toward my black belt. I am also an expert in weapons and self-defense. Throughout the years I competed on many different levels in multiple fights, and won many medals and championships.

Without realizing it at the time, martial arts kept me sane, and it was like therapy for me – and it still is. It has saved me from myself.

Through my studies of martial arts, I have learned some valuable life lessons. Above all, self-control and self-discipline: even though I have the skills to attack, it makes me the stronger and better person if I choose not to use these skills out of selfish motives. When you know the arts, they're meant to give you confidence in what you're capable of, so that you won't use it unless you have to defend yourself or your family.

Abdallah fighting in the USA

Of course, it took me a long time to really understand that and master it. When I was young, I was a troublemaker; if someone annoyed me, I would fight them on impulse, without caring who started it or how it happened. But as I grew in martial arts, I began thinking more and more about the implications of my actions and attitudes. The voices of my instructors were stuck in my head, reminding me: "Don't do it unless you have to!"

Living in a war zone makes it hard to define the line of impulsive offense and necessary defense. There are some circumstances or situations that occur, when you don't have much control over preventing or stopping a conflict; sometimes it is forced on you, and then you just have to fight. I had many of these kinds of fights as I got older.

One time, I was in a neighboring town that was the headquarters for the United Nations in our region, hanging out at a swimming pool with some friends, and an argument started that quickly got out of control. I don't remember much of what was said, but then someone intentionally splashed one of my friends who was sun tanning by the pool. "Hey, knock it off," my friend snapped. "Are you looking for trouble? 'Cause you're gonna find it!" In response, the guy got up in his face and splashed him even more.

Then everything went crazy. People were coming from all angles, jumping my friend and beating him. I saw the chaos erupt, and took a deep breath and said to myself, "Well, here we go!" I charged into action, grabbing and pulling people off him. Out of the corner of my eye, I saw a fist coming at me, but I blocked the punch and hit him back. One of my friends grabbed a big beer mug by the handle and hit another guy on the arm, giving him a deep and long gash. Chairs were flying through the air, and everything was a big mess, with a lot of property damage.

The pool owners had to shut down the pool and kicked us all out, but that just escalated the fight even more. The people who were fighting against us ran to their cars and grabbed their guns, so we did too, and we started chasing each other around the parking lot, shooting our guns. Then they left, and we thought it was all over, so we got ready to leave. But then we were ambushed – they had gone out and brought more people back with them, and they were waiting for us to let our guard down. They were

driving with machine guns, chasing us and firing at us. I hid behind a car, got my gun out, and started firing back. We were shooting at each other for at least ten minutes.

When news of our conflict reached the U.N. authorities, they rushed to the scene and dispersed everything. They came down with their weapons and got in the middle of the fight in the parking lot, and on megaphones they announced, "Everyone put your guns away! If you don't, we will have to open fire!" That put an end to the fight pretty quickly, but it didn't cool the tensions and hatred that had grown between our groups.

A few months later, when my wife and I were engaged, we went to visit her grandparents in that same town. There were people in that town who didn't want me to be there; we had fought some of them at the pool, so I was on their radar.

We were driving down the road, and someone was following us wherever we went, and all of a sudden he drove around us and cut us off. I didn't think much of it at first, beyond frustration that the driver was being careless and might cause an accident. Then he parked right in front of me, blocking the road, and wouldn't let me past, so I realized it was intentional and it was all planned. I beat the steering wheel and muttered, "Forget this, enough is enough." I got out of the car, went over to him and as calmly as I could manage, I asked him to move the car. He refused, so we started fighting, and I knocked him to the ground. Out of nowhere, about ten more guys came at me from every angle, with sticks, pipes, and cross-shaft wrenches.

My fiancé was in the car, watching all this happen, and she was terrified. I quickly looked around and saw that there was a wall behind me. "I need to protect my back," I thought, so I turned my back to the wall and started hitting people as they came at me. After four punches, I thought, "I'm gonna lose this fight, because this is too many people for me to take on alone." I knew they were trying to stop me from leaving town; they ambushed me and they had only bad intentions for me, and I felt trapped.

I was so upset, I lost it and jumped back in my car. I gripped the wheel and revved the engine. "I'm not gonna let them stop me. They're not gonna hold me down and do whatever they want to me. Here we go!" With that, I slammed on the gas and started driving through the crowd. People were flying off the hood, rolling over the top of the car on to the ground behind us, one after another, after another.

At the end of town there was an U.N. checkpoint, and if I stopped there, they could block me from leaving town and take me to jail. So I was determined to drive out of town as fast as possible. I flew through the checkpoint, and the U.N. officers jumped in their cars and chased after me, but they couldn't catch up to me.

We got back to our town, and I dropped my fiancé off at her house. Then I drove to my house and grabbed my machine gun. I prepared myself and thought, "Ok, I'm ready now. Whoever comes after me, this will be his last day on earth."

But the people who wanted to catch me did not pursue me once I was in my town; in fact, most outside people were afraid to come into my town, because we had a reputation of viciously protecting and defending our own people. Later on, I learned that at least five of the attackers were hospitalized with different injuries, from broken bones to cuts and bruises.

Life in a war zone is lawless, and the rules about fighting seem to mutate into a different beast. At times, the reality is that you either kill or be killed. The government won't judge you or protect you – you're in No Man's Land.

chapter 11

Finding and Losing Friends

I HAD THIS FRIEND GROWING UP, Tony, who joined the bomb squad when he was old enough. He did that for about five years, and he became the best at disarming bombs. He was the one they called in the most dangerous and complicated situations.

We weren't always friends, though. I remember when I was little, and he was sort of a bully in the school yard. He was older and bigger than me, over six feet tall. And he would laugh at me and make fun of my brothers. "You think you're so cool," he'd say, "but you are just a bunch of losers!"

"Oh yeah?" I turned on him. "Well, why don't you just say that to my older brother the next time you see him?"

"You and your brother, Joe - none of you scare me!" He laughed again as my face got red with anger, and my muscles tensed. But I knew I couldn't fight him alone... and I knew I didn't have to.

"Ok, I'll be back." I said coolly, and back-pedaled toward the road. "I'm gonna go get my brother!" I left the school yard and ran home. I found Joe, and told him about Tony and what he'd said. "He's waiting for you at the school," I concluded, "and he says he doesn't care."

Joe didn't hesitate. He stood up next to me and said, "Fine, let's go," and quickly stalked to the door. I ran behind the house and grabbed a long stick, then ran after my brother, who was already halfway to the school. I just loved that about my brothers. We were really close, always protecting and watching out for each other, fighting to defend our honor like a wolf pack.

When Tony saw Joe coming toward him, he started running away, and disappeared into the school building. The school was empty and abandoned, with most of the ground floor classrooms covered in shattered glass and debris from the bombings. But Joe spotted him and chased Tony through the classrooms. I wanted to help somehow, so I hid behind a door to one of the rooms, still gripping the stick. When Tony came into the room, I jumped out and beat him over the head with the stick, knocking him to the ground. Then Joe was there, and he jumped on Tony, and together we started beating him up, right there on the floor of the classroom.

Some of the other kids who were in the school yard ran away at the first sign of trouble – they didn't want to be associated with it at all. But a few of the kids couldn't help themselves. They were drawn to the fight, and stood around, shocked, watching to see what would happen.

I quickly realized this wouldn't be a fair fight. Even though he was bigger than us, it was still two against one, with Joe and I ganging up on him, so I backed off. I shook my stick at the boy on the ground and said, "See? I told you! I'm not gonna touch you, but I'm gonna let my brother teach you a lesson!"

After a few minutes, I started to feel bad for Tony, so I said, "Ok, Joe, stop now. That's enough! I- I think he's learned his lesson."

Joe got up, but continued to breathe hard, his muscles tight and ready for more. "Did you learn your lesson?" he growled at Tony.

Tony was cringing and moaning, but he quickly said, "Yeah, yeah, we're good! Now help me up!"

Joe reached out and grabbed one hand, and I grabbed the other, and helped him to his feet.

From that time on, Tony joined my brothers and me, playing soccer and hanging out in our gang. He became one of our best friends, and really was as close as family to us.

Tony married to a lovely girl named Rita. His brother-in-law, Gabby, was fascinated with the work that Tony did, and wanted to do the same thing. So he joined the bomb squad too, and they worked together. Tony trained Gabby, and Gabby enjoyed every minute of it.

Gabby and I were close friends for a long time, too. I owned two horses, a mother and her foal. I had always been fascinated by horses; their beauty and strength amazed and inspired me. But I found that it took a lot of time and effort to take care of them. When I started working full-time, my dad said, "These horses are too much responsibility, and you don't have time for it, and I won't do it, so you have to get rid of them!" We butted heads a lot over this issue, so finally I told him I would figure something out.

I learned that Gabby's dad had a farm, with sheep, goats and horses. So I asked Gabby if I could keep my horses at his farm. I paid him for the food and care, and it was a much better situation for everyone. Gabby took care of my horses, and we would go for rides together.

It was the most beautiful experience – to ride wild and free out on the rolling hills, where the battles and the destruction in the towns seemed very far away. We felt like two free birds, who had just escaped our cages. We would race each other out in the country, over those green fields, and just enjoy the escape from the war – the violence and tragedy of our lives -

for a short time. Out there, on the top of the hills, we breathed deeply the fresh air and looked down at the majestic scenery beneath us, as though we were kings who ruled it all.

"You know, our lives won't always be this way," Gabby said, squinting his eyes as he looked at the silhouette of our town on a distant hill. "Someday, I'm gonna leave the farm – leave it all behind. I'm gonna get married, and have a lot of kids – I want a big family, you know. And I'll be comfortable and successful – I'll have a good job that pays a lot of money, so I can have a big house and a fancy car..." He seemed to get lost in his fantasy for a few moments, so I just watched him and quietly waited. His eyes were looking at a world far away, and he had a hopeful smile that played at the corners of his mouth.

A distant roadside bomb exploded, and the sound of the blast echoed and ricocheted across the hills and valleys around us. It made our horses snort and stomp, and brought Gabby back to the present. "But most of all, I want to be free – free to live in peace and pursue my dreams."

"I know, my friend," I said. "But right now we can't afford to have dreams. We don't know what the future holds, or how much time we have. All we really have is today – right now."

"So if this is all we've got," Gabby said, "let's make it the best day of our lives. Instead of wondering and looking for things we don't know and can't see, let's just focus on what we have – live for this moment, and be grateful we're still alive."

"I agree. Live for this moment, and make it the best one yet," I said, nodding and reaching over to pat my friend on the back. Then I gripped my reins and pointed to an olive grove in the valley. "Hey, I'll race you to those trees!"

One day, Tony and Gabby were called to disarm a bomb that was found near the river. It was planted on a road where Israeli troops frequently travelled. When they arrived, they assessed the situation and started working on the bomb. But they didn't know that another bomb was hidden nearby. They also were unaware that an ambush had been set. The second bomb exploded, and suddenly there were bullets from every direction. Tony and Gabby, and the other soldiers who were with them, were all killed in a moment.

It was one of the worst days of my life, when I heard the news of their deaths. It was devastating to me and all who knew them. The grief was even worse for poor Rita, who had tragically lost her husband and her brother on the same day.

The funeral service for my friends was simple and brief. I helped to carry the caskets from the church to the cemetery nearby. Women wept and threw rice and flowers on the casket, and everyone wore black. Some men shot their guns in the air, in memorial to the young lives that were laid down, and as an expression of their emotions, a release of their pain and anger.

We never had time to process and grieve our losses for long, because the dangers surrounding us were always imminent. We had to remain vigilant, defending and protecting ourselves and our loved ones who were still with us... trying to prevent another death, another funeral, another tragedy.

chapter 12

My Rebel Ride

DID I MENTION I HAD A MOTORCYCLE? I didn't know anything about motorcycles – nobody had one in our town. All I knew was that they were fast and dangerous, and that was enough for me. I liked to pushed the limits and live on the edge, and this seemed like the best way to do that.

So I went to Beirut, found a dealer, and I said to him, "I want to buy a motorcycle!"

He looked at me skeptically and responded, "Do you know how to ride?"

"No." I gave my answer with a smile and without hesitation, a glint in my eye that dared the man to challenge my reckless judgment.

"Where are you gonna learn how to ride?" he asked next.

"I don't know," I admitted, shrugging my shoulders without much concern and looking around. "Here, I guess. Right in this parking lot."

"Are you kidding me?" the dealer snorted and crossed his arms, looking at me like I was crazy. Yeah well, so maybe I was.

"No, I'm not," I said, then pulled out my wallet. "How much do you want?"

"Ten thousand," he said, his arms still crossed and a smirk on his face.

"Ok, here's your money," I replied, holding out the cash. "Let's go sign the papers now."

He was surprised and taken off guard as he mechanically took my money and led me to his office. We went over the details of the agreement and signed the papers.

As we walked toward my new motorcycle, I stuffed the papers in my pocket and said, "Ok, now, show me, what do I do? It's my motorcycle now, so I'll take full responsibility if anything happens. Just give me the basic instructions, and I'll figure it out."

"Alright, well," he sighed, and reached out to demonstrate, "you grab this clutch here, put it in first gear like this, turn the gas on, and just... go." He shrugged and threw his hands up, then backed up and watched me straddle the seat for the first time. "Keep your feet on the ground," he added, "and don't pick them up until you're stabilized."

I tried it slowly a couple times at first, around the parking lot, shaking nervously the whole time. But it went well, so I gained confidence. "Ok whatever, I've got this!"

I rode my new motorcycle all the way from Beirut back to my hometown, which was about four hours away. I was the first person to own a motorcycle in the Security Zone. When I arrived in town, I was instantly the coolest, most popular person around. My neighbors were shocked at what I had done, and they wanted to get their picture taken with me and my new motorcycle. Everyone wanted to be my friend, and to ride with me... well, almost everyone.

My parents did not share the enthusiasm of the rest of the town. In fact, my dad kicked me out of the house. "If you want to kill yourself, go do it somewhere else," he said, waving me off in disgust. "But it won't happen on my watch. I don't like it, and I don't approve of this."

I didn't care. I had me, myself and my motorcycle, and I didn't need anything or anyone else. I made a choice: it was my motorcycle or my family, and I chose my motorcycle. Deep down, I knew I was being stupid and rebellious, but it gave me such an adrenaline rush, I couldn't resist – I felt alive and free, in a way I never had before. It filled a void in my life.

A few days later, when my dad cooled down, my mom begged him to let me come home. She didn't like for me to be away. "I'll talk to him, he'll drive slowly and carefully!" she reasoned, and I promised her I would, even though I never really did.

I had about fifteen high-speed accidents on that motorcycle. I wanted to see how fast it would go, and it went incredibly fast - 240 kph - and I tried to maximize my speed. I set up drag races with cars, and would just fly. Because of the car, the wind, and the speed, my motorcycle shook. My jacket would fill with wind, like a parachute, and I thought I would be blown away! By the grace of God, I escaped being killed many times.

Then, radical militants began to send suicide bombers into the Security Zone on motorcycles and killed many Israeli soldiers that way. So the Israeli Army sent out a memo to all the towns in the South: "No motorcycles are authorized in the Security Zone." But I didn't care. I was sick and tired of people telling me what I could and could not do, limiting my rights and freedoms.

A week after the memo was circulated, I was getting on my motorcycle when I heard one of my neighbors call out to me from across the street: "Hey! Guess what the Army says about motorcycles!"

"Hey!" I yelled back, "guess who's not listening!" and I started my noisy engine and sped off before they could say more.

The civil administration in my town sent me notes after that: "What are you doing? You know this is dangerous! Stop this now!" And I continued to ignore them.

One day, I was riding my motorcycle in a neighboring town, speeding so fast that I barely had time to slow down when I saw an Israeli convoy on the side of the road, aiming all their guns at me. I slammed on the brakes and the motorcycle skidded around in a circle on the path. I heard the commander shouting, "Don't shoot! Don't shoot!" He jumped out of the jeep and ran toward me, all the time waving his arms at the troops to hold their fire.

Then his yelling turned on me: "What are you doing? Are you crazy?

Do you want us to shoot you? You know you are not allowed to ride your motorcycle here!" His face was red, and sweat and spit were flying everywhere. "You are unbelieveable – I've had it with you! Any of them – *all* of them – could have pulled the trigger just now and you would have been dead!" He stalked around me, shaking his finger in my face and gesturing wildly, as he ranted like he was my own father. "You're always pushing your luck; you're trying to kill yourself!"

I pretended not to hear him, as I picked up the motorcycle and waited for the oil to settle back down. I got back on and started the engine, even while he continued yelling at me. "Whatever!" I yelled back and revved my engine in defiance. "I don't tell you what to do in Israel, so don't tell me what to do in Lebanon!" And with that, I spun my tires, spraying gravel and dirt at the convoy of soldiers and the commander who cared so much about me, and I left.

Then I was summoned to a committee meeting. When I showed up, they said simply, "You have to end this. You're taking too many risks. We don't want to see you get killed. You have to stop riding that motorcycle."

"No one is gonna stop me," I said defiantly. "I'm not gonna stop riding. I have the only motorcycle in this doomed area – they know the make, model, and color of it, and they know where I go. They can tell their soldiers anything they want, whether to protect me or shoot at me. But I'm gonna keep doing what I want."

Clearly, they weren't happy with my response, but they knew I was stubborn. I was careless and reckless, demanding that on this one point, they do what I wanted, not the other way around. And deep down they knew they weren't right to try to stop me; normal people in normal places don't live under such extreme restrictions. So they finally gave up, and I knew they wouldn't target me. I kept riding, and Israeli soldiers kept shooting warning shots over my head, but I knew they were just attempts to scare me. I was untouchable and unstoppable.

My brothers all wanted to learn how to ride, too. So one time when I was out of town, they seized the opportunity to ride my motorcycle around without me. The problem was, they rode it for too long with low oil in the engine, so the engine got messed up. When I got back, I was mad, but most of all, I wanted to get it fixed.

I'd heard about a motorcycle mechanic who had moved down from Beirut, so I called him to see if he could help. He came and got the motorcycle, and said it would be ready later that night. But, later that night, I didn't hear from him and couldn't find him anywhere. I called a friend to drive me to his town nearby, and we asked around about him. "Oh yeah, him," someone responded. "He's at the hospital. He was out driving a motorcycle around town – doing wheelies and messing around, kinda crazy – and he crashed. I think he's in critical condition."

We found out later that he had broken his arm, and had to have several metal rods put in his hand and shoulder. I felt really bad for him, but he brought it on himself.

I found my motorcycle, which amazingly was still in working condition, and decided to drive it back home. It was late at night, and very dark, so I couldn't see very far in front of me, especially since I was cruising along at my normal super-speed. Sure enough, there was a pothole in the road, and as I came around a corner, my front wheel hit the hole and threw me off, high into the air and several meters away, into a ditch filled with mud and water. I didn't take the time to consider how amazing it was that I hadn't cracked my head open or broken my neck; I just got up and got back on the motorcycle, all wet and muddy, and drove the rest of the way home as though nothing had happened.

That was my last real ride on the motorcycle. The mechanic had only half-fixed it, so every time I tried to start it up, it broke down again. The only place I knew of that would repair it was in Beirut, but by that time, I was a wanted man, so I couldn't risk it. My motorcycle days had finally come to an end.

chapter 13

A Different Kind of Shooting

WHEN I WAS IN HIGH SCHOOL, I applied for a job at a television station in Lebanon. There were not many jobs to be had in our town; most local businesses were family owned and run, and I didn't want to work in the fields like my dad. I wanted to be independent, to work hard and earn my own living. The television station was hiring at the time.

The building was surrounded by a very high concrete wall, with barbed wire around the top. Two guards stood at all times at the entrance, and the only vehicles that were permitted to pass inside or outside were the manager's car and the vehicles used for going out and covering stories. The manager had his own security escort that met him at the border and took him to the station. The station had all this special security and precaution because their coverage of the war was not censored or approved by the powerful forces that attacked and occupied our land.

My application was accepted, and I got an interview with the manager, Steve, a couple weeks later. As we talked, he said to me, "You know, your English is pretty good. Would you be interested in learning to do production to cover the war?"

"Yeah sure," I said without hesitation, "why not? I'd love to!" I had no

experience with anything related to media; until that time in my life, all my efforts had gone into becoming a fighter. But a job is a job, so I decided that whatever job was offered to me, I would take it and give it my best effort.

Steve wanted me to work as a cameraman, but I had no clue how cameras worked. Today, everyone has cameras, even on their phones; so it isn't a big deal, anyone can film things. But back then, cameras were not just lying around. I felt a huge responsibility to learn as much as I could, as fast as I could. I wanted to impress my co-workers and prove that I was the right person for the job. For about the first month or so, I went to work early in the morning, at 5:00, and stayed until 3:00 the next morning, just to play with the camera and figure it out so I would be able to use it well. It

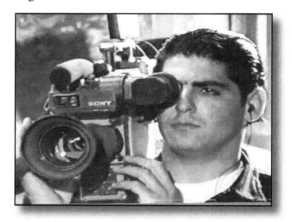

was a very intense time for me, teaching myself and figuring out everything on my own.

When I knew I could film without problems, I asked if I could go out with the camera crew to see what they did. Steve said, "Sure, do whatever you want. In fact, whatever you want to learn in this place is yours; just do it." When he said that, I felt like it was Christmas day; I couldn't believe he was going to let me use all the expensive equipment in the studio! The beta cam alone was worth $30,000. I wanted to work hard and learn everything about it, so I could really enjoy it and use it in the best way possible.

The camera crew started to help me when I joined them, but when they saw what I could do they were shocked, "How did you learn how to do

*Covering the late French President Jacques Chirac's
visit to Lebanon*

all this in no time?" Steve was impressed too. At first, he asked me to film minor things, like local celebrations and interviews, that they may or may not put on the air. But I did what he asked, and did it with all my heart, and Steve said, "Man, that is good! You're going to be great." I started asking if I could go out on my little assignments by myself, and he said, "Yeah, go ahead." I started developing confidence in myself and my filming skills, and

Covering the war in Lebanon

then I became the primary cameraman at the station. Pretty soon, I was covering everything else.

My time working as a journalist and videographer gave me opportunities to meet presidents, vice presidents, and other high ranking officials from around the world.

But I didn't stop there. I thought to myself, "You know what? I learned this thing, and I know I can learn more. I want to move on and learn what these editing machines do. There are a lot of buttons..." Again, I spent countless hours, day and night, working at the machines, trying to figure it out. There was no one to train me, no mentor or teacher to sit beside me and explain things to me. There were some manuals, so I studied the manuals and just tried things until I understood. Within three months, I was eager to edit.

When I asked Steve if I could edit, he looked at me with some surprise, "Do you know how to edit?" I just grinned and said, "I learned." "Show me," he said and walked with me to the editing suite. I sat down right then and there and showed him how I could use the machines, and he said, "Man, you are good! Ok, when you don't have anything to film, I want you to edit."

Directing live news in Lebanon

So I filmed and edited, and got really good at that. Then I thought, "I want to learn more... I like how things are done in the directing role, so I'll learn how to do that next." So, I learned that, and became good at directing. There were not a lot of people who worked at that station, just enough to count on your fingers. I decided to learn as much as possible so I could help wherever there was a need. I learned how to make graphics and do audio mixing, so by the time I'd spent three years at the station, I was able to do anything and everything in the control room.

I was great at what I did, and took much pride in myself. This was fulfilling me and changing my life forever. This was where I was going to shine. I'd never had an opportunity like that before, the chance to prove that I could be something special and be a part of something important. It filled a void in my life, and it was a healing process. It made me believe that life was not all about death, destruction, fear, and sadness; no, there is good in life, and I wanted to focus on that.

This next chapter contains real and disturbing images of war.

chapter 14

War Stories

Covering the 2nd Iraqi War

ALL OF A SUDDEN, I found myself in the middle of the battlefield. It felt so surreal, like a nightmare. I was thrown into the thick of war as though I were a seasoned warrior, but really I was flustered and disoriented. Every day at my job was different and had its own adventures. I felt like I was playing Russian roulette, pushing my luck with each story I covered. Every day was a new and tragic event. And instead of shooting guns to kill, I found myself shooting video of the war, to reveal the truth to the world. I loved and craved adventure, so I enjoyed the challenge and this level of professionalism in the face of extreme violence, but I struggled to make sense of everything I saw.

It was incredibly dangerous and risky; I almost got killed countless

With the US Troops in Baghdad

times. There were times when I was filming, watching everything go down.One time I went on assignment to cover a bomb that went off in town and targeted an Israeli convoy. It killed and injured some of the soldiers in the convoy. As soon as I heard the news of the explosion I got in the car and drove to the location. When I got there, I took the camera out of the car and started filming. I was just a few feet away from the soldiers. Of course, my presence was not welcomed by the troops on the ground, they were so distraught and frantic. They started yelling at me: "What are you doing here? You need to get out of here now!" One of the soldiers charged at me with his M-16 and shoved it against my chest with his finger on the trigger. I knew that he was dangerously close to shooting me if I didn't comply with their demands.

Throughout the whole altercation, we were standing next to a second bomb that was planted a few feet away from us in a pile of rocks on the side of the road. The bomb was molded in the shape of a rock so none of us noticed it.

I said, "Calm down, I'm just doing my job." The solider was not so happy with

In Iraq

my response. Again he pushed his machine gun against my chest. I took the camera off my shoulder but left it recording. All of a sudden, the bomb went off right next to me, killing and injuring all those who were in front of it. The soldier who had confronted me, pushed me far enough to get me out of the shrapnel radius of the bomb. I was the only one to walk away without a scratch. And I got the whole thing on tape.

I have tasted death many, many times. For ten years, my life was a continuous series of close-call encounters. If I were to write about them all, they would fill many books.

I was at the station one day, editing some footage for that evening's news report, when the office telephone rang. "Hey man, I thought you should know there's been an ambush." I often got calls with information about attacks, so I could cover the stories for the news station. Because of the intensity of my job, I always kept my camera in the jeep and was ready to go at a moment's notice.

When I drove out to assignments, I flew. I was always trying to break my personal speed record. I wanted to get there before things died down, because if I didn't, then I wouldn't have anything to film. It was a race against time, to be there and have something to cover. I glanced at my watch as I started the engine, and made a quick calculation: *The last time I went to this location, I got there in 20 minutes, and it was a rainy, muddy day... I know where the potholes are now, so this time I could probably get there in 17 minutes.* I mashed the gas pedal hard to the floor and roared down the street, going way over the speed limit, too focused on the story to even pray for safety.

As I got close, I heard shouting and machine guns, and was so distracted, trying to find the source of the chaos, that I almost crashed into the Israeli military personnel carrier, which was parked in the middle of the road. I saw it just in time to slam on the brakes, stopping just inches from the tank.

I could see soldiers on both sides of the road, scrambling for shelter behind cars and in ditches, all the while shooting blindly back and forth. I grabbed my camera and dodged from my car to the back of a tank, then dove into a ditch and followed behind some Israeli soldiers.

They couldn't figure out where the radical militant soldiers were firing from, but bullets kept coming from all sides and angles. Some of the soldiers began to notice me, but they were too busy trying to protect themselves and fight to even bother kicking me out.

Against my survival instinct, I crept closer and closer to the violence, capturing on film the bullets that found their targets, hitting Israelis and causing them to jerk and crumple to the ground. The fire exchange continued all around me, and I can still hear the sound of the bullets flying over my head: *Crack! Pop-pop! Tut!* But I still couldn't see the faces and the blood, so I inched ever closer.

As I scanned the area through my lens, I focused in on one Israeli soldier who was trying to get out of the crossfire and run away. *Tut-a-chut!* He had been wounded, and his leg was shaking so badly that he couldn't stand on it. He was coming toward me, and he slipped and fell, and tried to pick himself up, but just looked at me. Israeli soldiers don't usually let people get anywhere near them, especially in a war zone. Everybody is a threat to them, everybody wants to kill them, so they tend to shoot first and ask questions later. This man scowled at me with pain and demanded, "What are you doing here?"

"I'm filming!" I said to him. *Pop! Crack!* "I'm just filming!"

He was so upset and angry, he told me to leave. But I ignored his demands and continued filming as bullets flew over my head.

The attack continued for another fifteen minutes. When the shots subsided, I saw some of the Israeli soldiers emerging from the ditches. They were stooped, looking for the wounded and the dead, pulling them out of danger, assessing their condition.

That day I felt invincible, and I had so much pride for what I did. I felt like I could get away with anything, and I felt I could do things others wouldn't dare to do.

The adrenaline rush that I got from these moments became like a drug, and I got hooked. It was like I became addicted to the sound of gunfire, like the explosions were something I needed to see to feel alive. When the excitement would settle down and the rush would come to an end, I just looked ahead to the next day, the next attack, for my next fix.

Sometimes when I went on an assignment, I would stay out all night on the battlefield, while the troops were trying to extract soldiers who got ambushed, or they were going between towns with information about the fighting in other towns, or setting an ambush for radical militants, waiting

Israeli Casualties

all night long. Often I didn't carry food or extra supplies with me, thinking it would only last an hour or two, but then it went on and on, and I found that it was so dangerous that I couldn't leave, I couldn't go back home or back to the station. There were many cold nights that I stayed with the troops, experiencing their tension, fear and weariness with them.

The next day after the ambush, there were reports about a high-ranking Commander visiting the location where the attack on his troop took place. I grabbed my equipment, hurried to the car, and headed out.

When I got to the location, I saw the commander with his large entourage of soldiers who provided protection for him. They spread out around us, with their guns loaded and ready, searching trees and rooftops, anticipating another ambush. I turned on the camera and began filming, following the commander as he walked toward the troops.

Hezbollah Fighters

Suddenly there was a bright flash and a loud blast – *BAM!* – in front of me that threw me off balance and made my camera jostle. Where a soldier was standing just a second before, now there was a thick spray of dirt and debris and smoke, and the man was on the ground screaming and clutching his bloody stump of a leg. Someone yelled, "Ambush!" and everybody

Israeli Casualties

dove for cover, thinking they were under attack. But when they didn't hear gunshots or other explosions, they realized the man had stepped on a landmine. I kept filming, taking in the panicked look on his blackened face, and the brave men who moved forward to help him. His blood flecked my lens, making it harder to focus clearly, but also indicating how close I was to the explosion.

It was difficult enough to witness the agony and terror of the soldiers who fought in the war, but what was worse was seeing how the same violence affected civilians. This was a dangerous part of my work, too; it is one thing to show images of trained soldiers in battle to the world, but it is much more controversial to show the slaughtering of unarmed innocents. And too often, this is what I had to do.

A car bomb exploded this afternoon, killing a woman and her child, and injuring the taxi driver...

I was five minutes away when I got a call that a car bomb had exploded in a taxi. When I arrived at the scene, a crowd was gathering, and some soldiers were trying to pull the victims out of the car. I didn't have time to stare, I just hoisted my camera up and started filming the scene. Witnesses were talking all around me:

"I know that woman! She is my neighbor! Is she going to be ok?..."

"Sometimes I take care of her little boy. But I know he's been sick lately..."

"I think I heard her tell the taxi driver that they needed to go to the hospital..."

The soldiers got the door off the taxi, and first they managed to get the woman out. But she was most certainly dead, severely burned. Then gasps and cries arose from the crowd as a soldier lifted the little boy from

Lebanese Civilian Casualties

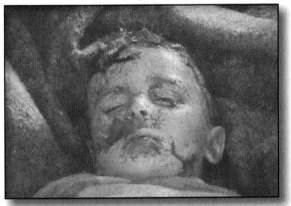

the wreckage. His face was torn, and a piece of his head was missing. He lay completely limp in the soldier's arms, and the man carefully laid him on the sidewalk and covered his small body.

My heart pounded as I took it all in, through the lens of my camera. What horrible atrocities! How could anyone be so cruel, so brutal?

I've seen so many terrible things that nobody should ever see: families buried alive under the rubble of their own homes, children dismembered. A lot of terrible images are etched in my thoughts, and have haunted me all my life, images that still today, I cannot wipe out of my memory.

Even after I left Lebanon and moved to America, I was very troubled. I struggled with depression, anxiety, and anger – all part of what psychologists call PTSD – post-traumatic stress disorder. I was angry at the enemies who attacked us and angry at the world, and I was angry at God for allowing so many terrible things to happen to my country.

chapter 15

Preparing for Change

I WORKED FOR THE STATION FOR TEN YEARS, covering the war news. They promised that if I stayed with the company, they would take care of me. But I was planning my own exit strategy: I would leave Lebanon before the situation got out of control.

That seems crazy, because there was a civil war going on – the situation had been out of control for as long as I could remember! And my job was incredibly dangerous, cheating death so many times, day after day. I would leave the station, never knowing if I would return in one piece, so how could the company really promise to take care of me? As time wore on, Israel's military casualties were increasing so much that they would be forced to retreat. Once the protection was lifted, we would be exposed to terrorists who wanted to kill us. I knew this time was coming.

So I was planning ahead, to escape before it was too late. I tried to explain this to my manager, Steve, one day: "I want to leave. I can't stay here. It is becoming too dangerous for me and my family."

But Steve pleaded with me, "No, no! You can't leave me! You are doing everything here – the filming, writing, reporting, editing, directing, producing! If you leave, I will have nobody! I'll have to hire multiple people to take your place, and I can guarantee they won't be as committed to their work as you are. Besides, no one wants to work here, especially if it becomes so dangerous that even *you* leave!"

He was right, of course. The station was a target for radical militants, because of our coverage of the war. Most of the Arabic media in the Middle East serves as a mouthpiece for radical militants, to spread their hateful messages and propaganda. Reports of innocent civilian casualties were never mentioned or highlighted. Western media followed and promoted the same propaganda. Yes, we were playing a dangerous game, and we knew it would catch up with us soon.

We were forced to leave Lebanon under gunfire on May 24, 2000.

Overnight, the Israeli Army decided to withdraw from South Lebanon. The next morning, I heard that news, and I knew our time was up. I'd called my wife and told her, "Get ready; we're leaving."

"Leaving?" she asked, and I could tell by her tone that she was confused, or maybe afraid to understand my words. "Leaving where?"

"Just- I don't have time to explain now!" I said, frustrated and worried as I watched more Israeli convoys roll steadily south. "The Israelis are leaving Lebanon, and we need to run to the border, too."

When I got home, my wife and baby son were waiting for me, but she wanted to go to her parents' house to be able to say her last good-byes.

"We don't have time," I said, trying not to look into her tearful eyes. "If we take that risk, we might not make it to the border. They could kill us at any moment!" I knew that was a terrible and difficult thing to accept. What if we never got to see our families again? I simply could not let the weight of that thought sink into me at that moment. We had no choice - we had to go.

I had to take my wife and my son, who was seven months old, and put them in the car and drive to the Israeli border, which was about 25 minutes away, with my machine gun sticking out of the window. My car was literally flying off the ground – that's how fast I was going, because I knew the situation was extremely serious. The radical Muslim groups were coming into town and killing the Christians - shooting them, executing them. Radical militants on motorcycles and in cars with weapons were everywhere. Our tiny window of opportunity was closing, so I didn't want to put my family in more danger than we already were.

When we got to the border, there were many other people there who were trying to flee Lebanon out of fear as well. There were around 4,000 people, packed in a narrow corridor and stuck between two worlds – on one side was the Israeli border, and on the other side was the Lebanese border. There were a lot of cars, and in front of the cars, there were a lot of people, and I was at the back of the line with my family. *There's no way on earth we're gonna be able to cross before they get to us.* That was my biggest concern as I quickly glanced behind us and ahead of us. *This is the end of the road for us, this is where everything ends – this is where we're gonna get killed. We can do nothing but give it a shot, and just start walking.*

We got closer to where the people were, at the back of the line, and then something really miraculous happened: the people started moving. You know how God split the Red Sea for Moses? People were giving us their spots, even though they were dying to get to the gate. One after another, they were moving to the sides of that narrow corridor, letting us come through. And in no time, I was approaching the gate. I was amazed: *This is not happening! How did this happen? From being at the end of the line to being right at the gate!*

On the other side of the gate, there was an Israeli general I knew from my time filming and reporting in Lebanon. I had known that general for a long time, and he was a good friend of mine. When he saw me at the gate, he said, "You and your wife and your son can go through, because I know you, so you can pass."

At that moment, the radical Muslims got to a higher level, and started shooting at us with machine guns. People started running, scrambling, trying to hide, to take cover. On the other side, the Israeli army was there, returning fire. And we were caught in the middle. The exchange went on for ten minutes, before they neutralized the terrorists and everything settled down.

Then the general told us again that we could pass. I was one of the first people, with my family, to get across to the Israeli side. We got across, but as I looked back, I realized that so many others were still waiting in that narrow corridor. There were a lot of people from my hometown. *It's not fair that I have favor, and leave them behind.*

I said to the general, "You know, you shouldn't be keeping people out. You saw what happened. You should let everybody come across the border."

"I can't let them go across," he replied, "because they want to get in with their cars, and we don't know what is in the cars. There might be something suspicious, and even dangerous, so we can't let people go across unless we get clearance from the Israeli government."

I understood this dilemma of security, but I was still thinking of the innocent people who would not be safe because of the time-consuming precautions. Then I thought of another option: "Why don't you give the people a choice? If people want to cross without their car, they can cross. That way you save their lives, rather than making them wait. I don't care if I have my car, and I don't care about material things; I just want to get my family safely across, and this is what everyone back there is probably thinking, too."

He said, "No, not everybody is like that. They're insisting upon getting in with their cars."

Again, I asked him to give the people a choice. "Those who really are desperate to leave will take the opportunity, even if they have to leave all their possessions behind."

The general considered this for a moment. Then he shrugged and nodded, and got on the PA speaker and announced: "People who want to get across without their cars can pass."

Immediately, we saw some of the car doors opening, families emerging, parents carrying their babies and holding nothing but their children's hands. As they walked forward together, more people followed their lead, and soon all the cars in the corridor were abandoned. People chose to leave behind all their material possessions for the sake of their safety, freedom, and lives.

By the time we all got across to the Israeli side where we were safe, the radical militants had reached the cars that were left behind. People had fled from their homes in a hurry just like we did, and had grabbed whatever they could, that might have value – jewelry, cash, clothes, and identification and other important documents. We watched from a distance as these things were recklessly thrown out of the abandoned cars and destroyed or stolen. So much was lost, but we all got out in time.

The Israeli soldiers gathered us in an area where they put us on buses and drove us to different parts of Israel. The bus was hot and crowded and tense; everyone huddled close, but were lost and isolated in their own thoughts and emotions.

I held my wife and my son, overwhelmingly grateful that I had been able to get them to safety, relieved that we were no longer in imminent danger. Thank God! It was a miracle that we were alive and together.

Then I looked over my shoulder, out the dirty back window of the bus, to the border of my homeland that was quickly fading away. The only home I had ever known, and the place that held all my childhood memories. *Will I ever return? Will I ever see my parents again?* A piece of my heart was firmly planted in Lebanon, and the rest of my heart belonged to my wife, my son, and my secret dreams. And as that bus carried me further down the dusty, bumpy road, I felt my heart, stretched to its limit, tear in two and I believed it would never be whole again. Life in Lebanon left me with a lot of scars, scars that cannot be seen. It was hard for me to grasp that I was really leaving Lebanon, and I didn't know if those scars would ever heal.

I turned and looked ahead at the road before us, as my thoughts also turned to the future. *What are we gonna do? How will I feed my family? Where will help come from? How long will this war last? Where will we live?* Once the questions started, they came like an unrelenting flood, pounding me with anxiety and helplessness – so many questions, with no answers in view.

I tore my eyes away from the road, to observe our fellow passengers on the bus. There were people I recognized, neighbors and family friends, who had picked olives with my parents, who had played soccer in the schoolyard with me, who had danced at our wedding. Now they were shell-shocked, feeling abandoned and vulnerable after the hasty retreat of the Israelis and the rapid advance of dangers that nipped at their heels as they fled. They appeared to be frail and fearful at this moment, but I knew deep down that as a community, they had a strong, resilient spirit – I had seen it many times before. We had lived in war and fought and defended each other most of our lives, and we were still here. This new challenge would not break us or be the end of us. We would keep fighting, until we had peace and security and a better life for our children.

Our children... I looked again at my baby son, Pedro, and even in the midst of my heartbreak, I couldn't help but smile at him. Because of my risks and my fight, he had the chance to truly live. He could grow up, not worrying about if he would eat dinner, have a warm bed, go to school from day to day. He wouldn't have to carry the fear and anxiety and uncertainty that weighed me down as a child. He could laugh and rest and dream and hope.

chapter 16

Back to Uncertainty

OUR BUS STOPPED ON THE SHORE of Tiberias Lake, or what was known in history as the Sea of Galilee. It's in the wilderness, where there is nothing but trees and rocks and water. We all climbed out, and at first I thought it was just a rest stop, somewhere to stretch and sort out a plan, and then we would be taken to a nice hotel, where we would surely be taken care of. But the bus left us there, and the sun went down, and with it went our chances of finding shelter; the air grew cold, the bus didn't return, and there was no one to explain what was happening or what we should do.

This is it, I finally thought. *This is as far as we're gonna go. We're on our own.* My wife and I had a duffel bag, with a little formula and a few diapers for our son, so we unzipped the bag and put Pedro inside, to protect him from the cold. We didn't sleep that night. We shivered from cold, we huddled close together, we prayed, and my wife cried. She mourned the fact that she had left Lebanon without saying good-bye to her parents, and this had been the longest time and the farthest distance she'd ever been away from them. Would she ever see them again? She wept over Pedro, fearing that he would freeze or starve in the night and she would have to bury him in the morning. What would she do then? How could she go on, after so much loss?

I tried to console her, like my dad had comforted me when I was a child. I heard his voice echo in my own, in words I said but could barely believe myself: "Things will get better... we're gonna make it, we'll be fine... God will not leave us... Trust him, and all will work out... *This shall pass...*"

The next day I walked around the camp, asking everyone I met if they had seen my brothers or my sister. This was one of the heaviest concerns on my mind; I didn't know if they had made it into Israel safely, or if they were even alive. Many buses at the border had taken thousands of people to all different corners of the country, and we were all eager to reconnect with our loved ones. I asked the people in our group about my siblings, hoping someone had at least seen them get on another bus at the border, but nobody had any information... nobody knew anything. We all hoped for the best outcome, but we found ourselves all back in that old, rusty uncertainty which eats away at life. Had we come this far, for nothing?

A while later, some Israeli commanders came to our camp and gathered us all together. "We did not expect this many people to come to our country all at once," they said, "but we are working very hard to find a place for you to stay and food for you to eat, while we sort everything out. We will do whatever we can to help you, but please be patient with us!"

The commanders walked around and talked with different people, listening to their concerns and trying to answer their questions. I approached one of them with my own questions that had plagued me all night: "What other parts of the country did the buses take people to? I need to find my brothers... Do you have a list of the people who crossed over yesterday? Do you have any names? Is there an account, a ledger, something I can look at to see if my brothers are here?"

"We're still going through the process of sorting everyone out and getting names," the commander said, as if for the five-hundredth time. "I'm sorry, but we have nothing to show you yet. We are still trying to count and register everybody and get all of that figured out, but right now we are just overwhelmed."

The next day, a bus came and took us all to a military camp in Haifa. The commander on the bus instructed us: "You must stay here until we figure out what to do. We don't know much yet about this situation, and it will take some time to sort it out. We need you to stay inside this military compound and not leave."

We knew we were kept in the camps for security reasons - our safety, but also the safety of Israel. All total, the number of Lebanese refugees who fled to Israel ended up being about 10,000 that month. They came in so fast and in such large numbers that it took weeks for the government to register and clear everybody. They didn't know who could be trusted to roam freely in Israel, because they didn't know who was who, what their background was, and what their intentions were as they crossed the border. No one was above suspicion, and everyone had to be vetted and accounted for. But being told we couldn't go anywhere made us feel like hostages, and sounded too much like our recent past, to provide any comfort. Nobody wants to leave one prison for another.

During those weeks at the compound, we stayed in small one-room apartments, and were given cooked meals in a common dining room. There was also medical care for the babies and children. The doctor came every now and then, but our camp held about 800 people, and everyone wanted to see the doctor, so he was overwhelmed. You were considered lucky if you managed to get a couple minutes with him to ask one question! Many people got sick, including our son. He had a high fever for several days, and my wife and I were sobered by the thought that we might lose him. I was finally able to talk to the doctor, and he prescribed a medication for my son, to bring down the fever.

Eventually, the government set up clinics around the camps to make medical personnel more accessible to us. They also eased off on the restrictions, and we were allowed to go outside the camp for recreation; buses took us on day-trips to the beach and the zoo. It took a while, but things slowly started to get better.

It took about a week for me to locate my brothers and sister, though the suspense and anxiety made it feel like months. They did get across the border safely, and were in camps scattered around the country. When I received news of them, I experienced such relief! I thanked God, and immediately felt a heavy burden lift from me.

I was also able to buy a phone card and make a few phone calls, one in particular to Steve, who had been in Cyprus since the Israeli withdrawal. He showed up a couple weeks later at the military camp, looking for me. He had promised to take care of me if anything happened, and he was there to fulfill that promise. "Are you ready to get out of here?" he asked me. "I can get you to the U.S., if that's what you want."

Ever since I got to Israel, I had been ready to leave and had been waiting for a way out, and more than anything, I wished to go to the U.S. In 1996, I'd been able to travel to America for a business conference, and since then I had hoped to make it my new home, where I could work, grow, have a future, and be free. Of course, Hollywood movies always help – everyone wants to go and live the American dream!

But I couldn't leave until I knew my brothers and sister were taken care of. They were still unsure what they were going to do, and they were waiting to find out where they would be welcomed. But soon after that, Germany granted political asylum for refugees, and my brothers and sisters decided to go. When they gave me this news, again I was relieved, and then I realized I was free – nothing was holding me back from going to America.

epilogue

Bright Light

WE LEFT ISRAEL FOR AMERICA on June 15, 2000 - my wife, my son, and I. I held our visas in my hand and stared at them with tear-filled eyes. But I wasn't really looking at the pictures or numbers, or even the signatures, which I still couldn't believe had been acquired so quickly. Instead, I was seeing something I had never really seen before – *a light at the end of my very long, very dark tunnel.*

It was a light I had believed in many years ago, when I was small and didn't understand the world, when the bright hope of my parents was sufficient.

It was a light I had watched become dim and nearly snuffed out in the cold dampness of the bunker, in the mutilating minefields surrounding my town, in the shattered windows of my education.

It was a light that I had fought to reclaim through bloodied knuckles, knock-out kicks, school yard fights, and parking lot shoot-outs.

It was a light that I fought to forget by playing dangerous games, recklessly speeding around on an illegal motorcycle, and capturing my nightmares on film.

And it was a light that I dared to pursue once more at the border of

127

my homeland - because no matter what terrors I witnessed and dangers I experienced, the light of hope refused to be quenched. For most of my life, it had been so overwhelmed by darkness that I couldn't see it, and so far out of reach that I couldn't touch it. And yet, now I could. It was small, and just a piece of paper, but it had my name on it. And it meant that I could live in a free country, and work and grow and raise my children without fear.

We didn't really know what we were walking into. We didn't know how hard it would be, once we moved to America – the complicated processes, the problems, the roadblocks, the headaches from simply trying to get adjusted, learning the system, finding an apartment, finding work, obtaining green cards... We knew the road before us was difficult and a little scary, but we also knew that we were moving forward on a new road that would lead to greater things.

In Lebanon, if we did anything, we didn't know if our actions would accomplish anything, would work the way we planned, or if we would even survive our best attempts. This made it impossible to dream; all we could do is live moment by moment. But in America, we could wake up each morning with a new and more positive outlook. I guess you could say we could see things in a different light... but for me, it was like seeing things in the light of hope for the very first time.

Made in the USA
Lexington, KY
17 November 2019